Theological Perspectives
on God and Beauty

THE ROCKWELL LECTURE SERIES
WILLIAM B. PARSONS, GENERAL EDITOR

The Rockwell Lectures constitute the oldest designated and now endowed lecture series at Rice University, Houston, Texas. Since 1938, when the inaugural lecture was delivered, the Rockwell Fund has generously supported the series. The lectures are dedicated to the general subject of religion.

In the series:

Beyond Liberalism and Fundamentalism
Nancey Murphy

Christianity and Civil Society
Robert Wuthnow

The Jesus Controversy
John Dominic Crossan, Luke Timothy Johnson,
and Werner H. Kelber

Reconsidering Nature Religion
Catherine. L. Albanese

Theological Perspectives on God and Beauty
John Milbank, Graham Ward, and Edith Wyschogrod

THEOLOGICAL PERSPECTIVES ON GOD AND BEAUTY

John Milbank
Graham Ward
Edith Wyschogrod

TRINITY PRESS INTERNATIONAL
A Continuum imprint
HARRISBURG • LONDON • NEW YORK

Trinity Press International
P.O. Box 1321, Harrisburg, PA 17105

*Trinity Press International is a member of
the Continuum International Publishing Group.*

Cover design: Corey Kent

Library of Congress Cataloging-in-Publication Data

Milbank, John.
  Theological perspectives on God and beauty / John Milbank, Graham
Ward, and Edith Wyschogrod.
    p. cm. — (Rockwell lecture series)
Includes bibliographical references and index.
  ISBN 1-56338-414-0 (pbk.)
  1. God—Beauty. 2. Aesthetics—Religious aspects—Christianity. I.
Ward, Graham, 1955- II. Wyschogrod, Edith. III. Title. IV. Series.
  BT153.B4 M55 2003
  231—dc21
                                    2003006492

Printed in the United States of America

03 04 05 06 07 08   10 9 8 7 6 5 4 3 2 1

Contents

1

Beauty and the Soul

John Milbank

MODERNITY AND THE ABSENCE OF BEAUTY

Beauty arises where the attraction exercised by a formed reality is ineffable and escapes analysis. We speak of "beauty" just because we cannot capture this attraction in a formula that would allow us to produce other instances of the beautiful. For the same reason, we cannot substitute an abstraction of essence for the concrete aesthetic experience.

Neither, on the other hand, does an exhaustive description of the object and the way it appears precisely convey our sense of its specific instance, though it may present a beauty of its own, and "bring out" aspects of the object's beauty that reside only in this secondariness.

So it seems that there is an excess in the experience of the beautiful. Beauty is indeed, as Aquinas says, "what pleases the sight"; it concerns desire for the good as well as knowledge of the true. Since we never entirely bring away from the object all its beauty, this implies that even when we stand before the beautiful object, we are "held" by something that binds us only in its not-quite arriving. To experience the beautiful is not only to be satisfied, but also to be

1

frustrated satisfyingly; a desire to see more of what arrives (nonetheless with the same specificity that renders this "more" problematical) is always involved. Therefore, the beautiful resides not only in the truth of the object but also in its goodness that is a kind of destiny of the object for the subject.

However, it is never a matter purely of desire for concealed goodness. We cannot abstract the desire and the teasing pleasure either. They do indeed exceed the apparent formed, proportioned integral object; yet they are the excess of *this* object, a luminosity immediately resultant upon the manifestation of the form. Hence our longing for the beautiful form seems to shine from it, situating us within its disclosed world that has its own new and surprising urges. This longing is not in our possession, but conveys an inexhaustible depth of object that belongs to it while exceeding it. The depth is a signal within the form of the object whose intention embraces us.

Given this simultaneous objectivity and subjectivity of the experience of the beautiful, we can say that to see (taking seeing as embracing all sensory and phantasmic experience) the beautiful is to see the invisible in the visible. Hans Urs von Balthasar rightly contends that the experience of "Glory" in the Bible—of a hidden divine source irradiating the finite surface—involves just this.[1]

In the High Middle Ages, the possibility and experience of seeing the invisible in the visible, or of seeing the invisible *as* invisible (this is the necessary other aspect), was generally assumed and pervaded life, art and understanding.[2] Therefore, there was no specific discipline of "aesthetics," which only arose in the eighteenth century. Beauty took care of herself.[3]

By contrast, one mark of modernity is that we still, indeed, acknowledge the invisible, yet we only stand on its brink, and only

---

1.   See Hans Urs von Balthasar, *The Glory of the Lord,* (vol. 1 of *Seeing the Form*; trans. Brian McNeil et al.; Edinburgh/San Francisco: T&T Clark/Ignatius Press, 1988).
2.   I am indebted here to conversations with Oliver Davies.
3.   The formula is Eric Gill's.

acknowledge it as unknown. We continue to see the invisible as invisible, but we have lost the counterpoint: seeing the invisible in the visible. In consequence, we only *see* the invisible as visible in the sense that we are blinded by it: seeing what we see when we close our eyes. Bedazzlement now no longer betokens an excess of saturated form. Thus Duns Scotus's famous rebuke to Dionysius: *Negationes etiam non summe amamus* misunderstands, certainly, the Dionysian hyper-positive divine provocation of negation of our highest conceptions (even of divinity itself) yet may apply, indeed, to the modern cult of the sublime.[4] Without this cult, we moderns remain agnostic concerning the unknown; with this cult, we hypostatize and consecrate the unknownness as the force of nullity.

In modernity, therefore, there is no mediation of the invisible in the visible, and no aura of invisibility hovering around the visible. In consequence there is no beauty.

Instead, there is the sublime: an experience of the ineffable and overwhelming, at the margins. Within the margins, by contrast, there flourishes a reduced beauty: at worst this is a "mere" prettiness (as opposed to a prettiness that is a true species of beauty), able to be guaranteed as reproducible with trivial difference following a procedure; at best this is—from Kant to the kind of purely abstract painting that in no sense shows the hidden or the real (Mondrian, perhaps)— mere design that, albeit without prescribed measure, relates only to the general formal capacity of the designing imagination.[5]

Before modernity, the sublime was an aspect of beauty itself—the terrible aspect that is the wounding excess of the visible that pierces our everyday defenses. Thus, no sublime/beautiful duality is found in Longinus, or in the Middle Ages, or in sixteenth- and seventeenth-century rhetorics and poetics after the revival of Longinus and Hellenistic rhetorical reflection in general. No rupture is yet apparent in

---

4.   Duns Scotus, *Ordinatio* I, d.iii.q.i
5.   See Phillip Blond, "Perception: From Modern Painting to the Vision in Christ," in *Radical Orthodoxy* (London and New York: Routledge, 1999), 220–43.

Boileau; it commences somewhat with Fénelon, and then with Burke, decisively, who bequeaths it to Kant.[6]

Kant remains the supreme theorist of the modern aesthetic.[7] He recognizes that the beautiful is ineffable. But he arbitrarily placed this ineffability on the side of subjective feeling alone. For given his view that the feeling of the beautiful indicates a free play between the faculties (of reason, understanding, imagination and sensation), there is no real way to isolate the respective contributions of sensation and imagination from cognition, and hence no real way to distinguish objective from subjective contributions. By his ungrounded preference, Kant reduced beauty to an *a priori* meta-category—already allied to pure abstraction (as his examples of "design" indicate) without mimesis or disclosure of depth, and *just for this reason* without real productive originality either. The "new" instance of beauty is, after all, a mere specific variant of the unaltering genus of meta-categorical free play between the faculties, which is always identical in its unremitting formality of lack of preference. Since the feeling of the beautiful is really the reflex encounter with this formality, it is not in any sense a feeling capable of original production. Because the beautiful objects only occasion this feeling, their novelty, though endlessly engendered, is also ceaselessly erased.

Moreover, this lack of real presence of beauty in the object also redounds upon the theoretical status of the object within Kantian thought. For while the free play of the faculties is an objective reality in its very freedom, and exercises a function that is essential even for theoretical cognition (a meta-aesthetic function in relation to the *aesthetics* of sensation involved in theoretical cognition—a function always present, which the experience of art only brings to the conscious surface),

---

6. See Debora K. Shuger, *Sacred Rhetoric: The Christian Grand Style in the English Renaissance* (Princeton, N.J.: Princeton University Press, 1988)—a book that should be carefully read by all who venture to talk about "the sublime." See also John Milbank, "Sublimity: The Modern Transcendent," in *Religion, Modernity and Postmodernity* (ed. Paul Heelas et al.; Oxford: Blackwell, 1998), 258–85.

7. See Milbank, "Sublimity," and Milbank, "The Soul of Reciprocity Part I," in *Modern Theology* (July–August, 2001): 335–91.

it nonetheless performs this role in an arbitrary fashion, revealing a lack of right behind the justified exercise of theoretical right. Prior to any theoretical grasp of objectivity, and as the pre-condition for it, the aesthetic judgment isolates a discrete object snatched from the continuum of time, and thereby actually occludes—as Kant astonishingly admits—the reality of this flux.[8] In this way it is only a transcendental deduction of the beautiful that completes the transcendental deduction of theoretical understanding, which otherwise remains problematically poised between an empirical object that is really fantasized or posited by the transcendental ego, or else a pre-established harmony between material appearance and the *a priori* laws of understanding.

Yet this completion is at a terrible price and does not really end the aporia of deduction (as idealism after Kant quickly testifies). For under the terms of this completion, discreteness of the object is itself not objective but the result of arbitrary imposition. Moreover, if the boundary between understanding and reason concerns just the possibility of schematizing the categories of the understanding in relation to the objective, then, since the objective is itself established by the free play of the judgment that we can only know in the feeling of the beautiful, then we derive a "limit" for schematization always in terms of the category of the beautiful. The beautiful in Kant secretly gives limitation to the object and so to theoretical reason as such, and the beautiful is in turn only limited—that is to say, confined to the finite—because of the division between the beautiful and the sublime. This division can no longer be related to the general theoretical principle of distinguishing between legitimate understanding and transgressive (or semi-transgressive) reason, because, on the contrary, as we have seen, the former division alone upholds the latter distinction. The suspicion consequently arises that the latter division is cultural and subjective rather than genuinely critical. Therefore, if this argument is true, the Kantian project itself founders if one can question the duality of sublimity and beauty.

8.   Immanuel Kant, *Critique of Judgement* (trans. J. C. Meredith; Oxford: Oxford University Press, 1989), 105–9.

Because "the beautiful" actually coincides with and secretly establishes the limits of theoretical understanding, it ensures that the ineffable excess of the aesthetic no longer points to the infinite, whether of transcendence or immanence. Or rather, this ineffable excess is bifurcated: on one side it willfully isolates an empirical object, which only then is "given" to sensory intuition; on the other side it indicates, through a surplus that must inhabit its violently arbitrary instance, the infinite of the sublime, which is interpreted by Kant as the gateway to moral reasoning.

Modern beauty after Kant is therefore a "raped" beauty. She appears only in that scene where she is violently surrounded and delineated, and desire for her arises not from her instigation, consent and production, but is wrenched from her as an entire appropriation of all her form to the (dis)interest of our feeling. Attention is immediately wrested away from her form and what it might disclose, to the scene itself, wherein alone she is allowed to be disclosed at all. Within this scene, the excessive gesture beyond the scene is taken away from her and granted to the perpetrator of objectivisation, whose will is not thereby exhausted, but resides securely within indeterminate terror in general. Too late, beyond the deed which violates the phenomenal (the entire bio-sphere), terror is recuperated by a mild will able to withstand it in the name of his own—yet equally everyone else's—non-incarnated freedom. This is the will termed "moral."

It is clear that this economy of sublimity and reduced beauty is the economy of the unknown hypostatized as the unknown. Here glory, or true beauty, as the appearance of the invisible in the visible, is directly refused. Therefore theology, not simply as one of its tasks, but in order to ensure that today there can be something theological at all, must, as Balthasar realized, seek to reinscribe the sense of the beautiful.

But if beauty concerns a mediation between the invisible and the visible, then it involves *reciprocity*. The invisible "gives" the visible (since it is in itself hypervisible), but the visible "returns" to the invisible (since it neither negates invisibility, nor in any sense adds to its sum). Or to put this inversely: the visible abandons (gives itself utterly) to the invisible, and yet the invisible returns to the visible its form and elevates this form in an eminent fashion. This "eminence" is proper to the invisible as such and is finally inaccessible to us *in via*; nevertheless, in being drawn into the depth of the visible, we are abstracted away from its immediacy, and yet in such a way that this immediacy is redoubled and intensified. We enjoy thereby some limited and yet increasing insight into eminence.

In contrast with this reciprocal interplay, modern and postmodern favoring of the sublime explicitly refuses reciprocity (Deleuze, Levinas, Marion)[9] and celebrates a one-way gift. Insofar as the invisible sublime arrives in the visible, it loses itself in a merely negative kenosis. Inversely, where the visible offers itself to the invisible, this is utter self-sacrifice without return.

It would seem, though, that the perspective of sublimity conjoined with unilateral gift is right. Between God and humanity there is no reciprocity: God in his transcendence can receive nothing from us. This cannot be denied short of idolatry. However, if God is not really related to us, it is still the case that we only exist at all in terms of our real relation to God (the denial of this real relation by Ockham seems to erect a space of being unproblematically external to God; but if creatures are only nominally related to God, as they might be among themselves, then God is reduced to ontic status).[10] We only receive existence, life, and reasoning from God in returning ourselves to God. Is this utter self-loss and dereliction? No, insofar as the divine movement to create is included in the very generation of the *Logos*, and therefore belongs (unfathomably) in its very freedom to the divine essence itself. So in returning, we are always again given, in our distinguished degree of participation.

9. Gilles Deleuze, *Difference and Repetition* (trans. Paul Patton; London: Athlone, 1994), 1: "If exchange is the criterion of generality, theft and gift are those of repetition"; Emmanuel Levinas, "The Trace of the Other" in *Deconstruction in Context* (ed. Mark C. Taylor; Chicago: Chicago University Press, 1986), 349: "radical generosity . . . requires an ingratitude of the other"; Jean-Luc Marion, *Etant Donnée: Essai d'une Phenomenoloqie de la Donation* (Paris: Presses Universitaires of France, 1997), 119.

10. William of Ockham, *Quodlibetal Questions* (2 vols; trans. Alfred J. Freddoso and Francis E. Kelley; New Haven: Yale University Press, 1991), *Quodlibet* 6. Q.8, *Responsio,* 2:518.

Yet there is a dimension beyond even this. To be fallen is to deny (like Ockham and his hierophants) the asymmetry of real relation: to deny (impossibly) that we exist only within our return. In the Incarnation, God, through his assumption of humanity, renders this return for us. Certainly he does so as the return of the human essence to the whole Trinity, but also he does so through a personification, a "dramatization" of this return (this is necessary since there is no unpersonified, free-floating human essence) as the return of the Son to the Father.[11] This return that reflects their unsunderable bond "exceeds" both Father and Son in its character of love that is the *donum* of the Holy Spirit, that forever creatively offers (with a certain constitutive unilaterality, since this "extra" is what ensures that the return is never identical) reciprocity beyond itself. Through the Spirit, the transformation of the human essence is made available to us; through the Spirit, we also, as merely human hypostases, are enabled to "personify" the return to the Trinity, within the community of really related persons that is the Church. But in order to do this, the gift of the Spirit must also bring us within the reciprocal interplay of Father and Son. With Christ, as also the Son, we return to the Father. Thus the impossible solution to the impossibility of fallenness is that, despite our createdness, there is now reciprocity between God and us. Through the utter outgoing of the Spirit, we are now caught up into the substantive relation of Son to Father. Maximus the Confessor affirmed this: God's gift to us is the gift of reciprocal interchange with God. For God in the Incarnation gave his divinity to our humanity, so divinizing it that we in turn can truly give our humanity back to God—not by finite addition, but insofar as we are caught up in that infinite supplementation that is the *Logos*.

To defend beauty against the sublime, therefore, is also to defend reciprocity against the unilateral. But a third dimension arises here also, which will concern us for the remainder of this essay. This third dimension concerns a defense of the *soul* against the modern *subject*

---

11. See Hans Urs von Balthasar, *The Action* (vol. iv of *Theo-Drama*; trans. Graham Harrison; Edinburgh/San Francisco: T&T Clark/Ignatius Press, 1980), 205–427.

and its radicalization as the postmodern dispersed subject. For the purveyor of a one-way gift enticed by no beauty, but only the sublime moral persecution of the invisible other, is also (as Marion indicates) the Cartesian subject immediately related to itself as given to itself in auto-affection and only interrupted in its autonomy by another subject, which, if deemed essentially invisible, must in consequence be conceived also as purely self-related.[12] The Cartesian subject naturally breaks through its solipsism only via self-sacrifice, the one-way gift. What is refused thereby (beginning with Descartes's *Second Meditation*) is the soul, which is not pure-invisible-presence-to-self, or invisible-presence-of-the-other-to-self, but rather the gathering up and specific interrelating of real forms, real shapes outside the body, as well as the shape of one's own body.

Since, in this fashion, the soul is already inter-objective, intersubjectivity poses no problem; it merely intensifies inter-objective interactions and ensures that encounters with psychic others also assume a form and a shape. Here the appearance of the other and the being of the other, since it is beautiful, does not form a totalizing barrier which requires one to invoke a "non-being"—thereby pressing beyond the bounds of sense, which is inevitably articulated concerning "that which is."

RECIPROCITY AND TOUCH

The later philosophy of Maurice Merleau-Ponty provides a threefold defense of beauty, reciprocity, and the soul—with the main focus on the third element of this triad. I believe that this makes him almost unique among twentieth-century philosophers, although I suggest that his vision requires a theological reworking to ensure consistency.

---

12. Jean-Luc Marion, "Does the *cogito* affect itself? Generosity and Phenomenology: Remarks on Michel Henry's Interpretation," in *Cartesian Questions: Method and Metaphysics* (Chicago: Chicago University Press, 1999), 96–118.

In presenting Merleau-Ponty, I shall develop an intertangled account of two texts: first of all, Aristotle's *De Anima,* which represents the premodern linking of soul and reciprocity. Secondly, Merleau-Ponty's late essay, "The Intertwining," which extends Aristotle's view (more than is admitted) into an already postmodern account of the post-subject, and yet, by bending back into the premodern Aristotle, goes beyond this to produce a post-postmodern account once again of the soul.[13] Whereas the post-subject is inscribed by linearity and irrecoverable loss, the revivified soul is inscribed by a spiraling circularity and asymmetrical return.

According to Aristotle, the soul is commonly thought to comprise motion, sensation, and incorporeity.[14] Following this scheme, we need first of all to understand how sensation is a folding back within the sensed itself, which mediates between motion (*kinesis*) and action (*energeia*). Secondly, we need to understand how incorporeal thought is a folding back upon itself of sensation.

Merleau-Ponty asks how it is that, although the only world we have is a world entirely covered by our gaze and caressed by our touch, we nevertheless gaze upon and touch things independent of ourselves and apprehend them as having a depth beyond our grasp? His answer is that our mind is not an ego looking through our body at what it sees. Rather, it is first of all our body itself that sees and touches. The body has a peculiar ontological status, because it is at once itself tangible, as Aristotle had already observed, and yet something that itself senses other things. It is both object and subject, and *must be* object if it is to be subject. Thus unendangered removal from things is not the first precondition of sensation; to the contrary, the first precondition is to be endangered among things. In order to sense, a thing must be capable of being sensed in turn; it is

13. Maurice Merleau-Ponty, "The Intertwining—the Chiasm," in *The Visible and the Invisible* (ed. Claude Lefort; trans. Alphonso Lingis; Evanston, Ill.: Northwestern University Press, 1968), 130–56. In the same book, see also "Interrogation and Dialectic," esp. 79–83.

14. Aristotle, *De Anima,* 405b 10–15; 430a 20–25, 15–20. For the English edition, see Aristotle, *On the Soul* (trans. W. S. Hett; Loeb Editions; Cambridge, Mass.: Harvard University Press, 1936).

committed to this circle. On the other hand, this is a never-completed circle. Merleau-Ponty adds to Aristotle that the subject/object alternation is repeated with the asymmetrical symmetry of the body itself: One hand can touch another. However, while a hand is being touched, its own touching power falls into latency. The circle is never closed, and the spiraling forever renewed.

A phenomenology of the body therefore shows that sensation is first of all a capacity of the sensible itself, albeit of a specially privileged class of sensible. The earlier Merleau-Ponty, in *The Phenomenology of Perception,* concentrated in "epistemological" fashion upon this special class of "bodies." However, the later Merleau-Ponty pursued a more ontological enquiry. This approach concentrates upon the point already mentioned: all that is appears, and yet somehow appears as not reducible to appearance. Merleau-Ponty, then, uniquely carries out a phenomenological reduction to the point where reduction and phenomenology are breached: More than appearance appears, but unlike Heidegger, Levinas, Derrida, and Marion, he does not hypostatize this appearing of the inapparent as reduced self-cancelling Being, the sublime or the saturated phenomenon. Nor does he cling (like Marion) to any Husserlian subjective sphere of immanence: instead, phenomenology opens out directly beyond itself into ontology. Yet, inversely phenomenology remains: As for the Platonic *dynamis,* the mark of being is an appearing from a hidden depth.

Within this perspective, it cannot be the case that first there are inert "objects" of sensation, and then there are sensing bodies perceiving them, as if this were a haphazard contingency. On the contrary, the only sensed things we know are the things that can be sensed, the things somehow destined to be sensed. But why, then, do we sense them as more than appearances, why is idealism counterintuitive? Here Merleau-Ponty seems to connect our sense of a depth within things sensed with the fact that, in sensing our own body, we remove ourselves from our own body into a reserved corporeal depth. This suggests that the realm of sensed things or sensations is a kind of two-dimensional screen or "pellicle" between the depth of bodies on the one hand, and the depth of objects on the other. In that case there is no dualism of sensed things and sensations, and we should cease to think in terms of the prime border being between the surface of our body and what lies outside it. Instead, the entire series of sensed things to which body belongs forms one continuous surface that Merleau-Ponty (following Aristotle though he does not say so) names "flesh." At the point of "bodies," flesh somehow folds back upon itself, becomes "for itself" as well as "in itself," and in being able to touch itself is also able to touch the whole series of fleshly things.

However, this is no simple materialism. The flesh is as much spiritual as it is material, because the showing of a depth of possibility that is spirit is constitutive of everything. Things do not exist as discrete solid items, but as networks of interconnections, remote echoes and indications, associations, "kinships," expectations and deferrals. Like the ancients, Merleau-Ponty takes the primary apparent as "color," and insists that *this* red is uniquely rendered red by its situation, its contrasts with other remembered reds (and so its particular situation upon a continuum), and its contrast with other qualities within which it is instanced. Here the real and the signifying are tangled up, and not just for us, but also *intrinsically* within an objective reality that is, however, also subjective reality. There are two never-interlocking circles: the one of the world that includes body within its cycle, and the other of the individual perceiving body that exceeds and jumps out of the first circle to form its own. Within the second circle, the world is equally included. But this inclusion is only possible because the depth within bodies also *is* the depth within things. There are not really two confronting depths mediated by a screen. Instead, the density of things that the screen of flesh shows is itself the unconscious fold within flesh wherein the conscious fold of perception can emerge. Things appear as separate from us, things that are not us appear at all because they are simultaneously resistant to appearing. What appears is a density, a not-showing, which is the depth of things. In seeing things we can inhabit this depth, which then becomes our depth, our distance from things, and even from our own body, within our body.

On this view, philosophy must return to an always secretly pre-supposed ontological depth where the sensed and the sensation entirely belong together, and the sensed folds back into sensation with uttermost primordiality. However, this was surely already the view of Aristotle. He talks about how "sound" has two faces that are yet inseparable—the sound heard and the hearing of sound. For him the voice (*phone*) and hearing (*akoe*) can be identified at some level.[15] Moreover, he also speaks about how, in sensation, the body forms one surface with the things sensed and names this surface "flesh" (*sarx*).[16]

Also in Aristotle the doctrine of flesh is a paradoxically spiritual or psychic doctrine: indeed more emphatically so. For Aristotle, the soul is the actuality (*entelechia*) of moving things. It is, as it were, what the seeing of the eye would be, were it hypostatized.[17] Or rather, it is like the faculty (*dynamis*) for seeing. However, absolutely, and even for the most part in time, actuality precedes potentiality, and both constitute and show what a thing is.[18] We know the eye in its seeing, not in dissection (hence modern science must forever miss the eye in its real *eidos*). Likewise, we know the soul in its moving of things, in its sensing, and sometimes in its knowing. Moreover, since we can know nothing of anything outside this sensing and knowing, we can take it that *psyche* is the *telos* of *phusis* herself.[19]

All self moving things must negotiate with the outside world, even if their movements are only of generation and nutrition. In this negotiation they must sense things in order to survive and increase. They must *touch* things, and touching always involves feelings of pleasure and displeasure.[20] In this way objective encounter is always also subjective, and Merleau-Ponty affirms this point in his own fash-

---

15. *De Anima*, 491b 4–10; 426a–416a 10.
16. Ibid., 423b 25–27.
17. Ibid., 421b 20–413a 4.
18. Ibid., 431a 1–5: "For everything comes out of that which actually is" (*esti gar ex entelechia ontos panta ta gignomena*).
19. Ibid., 415b 15–21.
20. Ibid., 414a 33–414b 17.

ion. For survival and increase, uprooted animals, wandering things, need to sense at a distance: hence they can also see and hear. But in all these cases, if the soul is first known in the actuality of sensation, then this in turn can only be understood in terms of the registering of an object.[21] To define the actuality of sensation, one must first define the object: for objective sound turns into subjective sound; objective sight into subjective sight and so forth. There is a teleological destiny here. This was why Brentano thought there was already a doctrine of "intentionality" in Aristotle, although the idea of a radical intellectual "return" to things really derives from Augustine.[22] Indeed, for Aristotle this can only be understood finally when we affirm that even vegetative and animal motion is a *methexis* in the immortal life of mind. He *does,* like Plato, have a doctrine of participation at this point.[23]

In the case of vision, this sensation is known through the object that is light. Light, declares Aristotle, is, in a sense, "the color of transparency."[24] Transparency is a pure medium of communication; it is simply what allows things to arrive at and from a distance. As such, it does not itself travel: Light cannot be in motion, and even today one must agree.[25] Light is not in motion because, as transparency, it is the spatial equivalent of the immediacy of the moment, which as the essence of passing time is yet snatched out of time as the folding of the past into the present and the present into the future. Likewise, light as transparency is the immediate presence of the "over there" in the "before me," which although it mediates discrete spaces, also exceeds their discreteness and so is the removal of space from space. Merleau-Ponty also regarded both time and space as somewhat like this. The "light" whose speed is measured by modern

---

21. Ibid., 412b 26–413a 4; 414a 17–19; 418a 3–8.
22. Dermot Moran, *Introduction to Phenomenology* (London: Routledge, 2000), 49–50, 54–55.
23. Aristotle, *De Anima,* 415a 30–415b: "For this is the most natural of functions among living creatures . . . to reproduce one's kind . . . in order that they may have a share in the immortal and divine in the only way that they can" (*in tou aei kai tou theoin metexosin e dunantai*).
24. Ibid., 418b 11–12.
25. Ibid., 418b 21–27.

(experimental) physics is only the machinery of particle or wave motion that somehow occasions the phenomenon of light, although the effect of light incomprehensibly exceeds this "cause." Modern physics does not attain to light as *eidos*. Light, however, is also a little more than transparency for Aristotle. The medium has its own faintly visible glow that alone renders things visible through the transparent. This glow is the presence of fire in the transparent that activates it and permits vision. Thus, "Color [fire] moves the transparent medium."[26]

Visibility, therefore, is defined as the full actualization of light according to its *telos* that resides in the *psyche*. Visibility is transparency, the miraculous crossing of distance that at once obliterates it and conserves it. Aristotle observes that the proximity of sensation must always preserve distance, because if an object is brought too closely up against the eye, it cannot be seen.[27] However, this does not appear to be the case in the instance of touch. Where, in this instance, is the medium that prevents blinding saturation? It is here that Aristotle, also, before Merleau-Ponty, interprets flesh (*sarx*) as the intervening medium between depths, or rather, as the allowance of the opening and folding back upon itself of the one depth.

For he declares that in the case of touch, the medium is not light or air (as for sound) but rather flesh itself: the surface formed between touching bodies. Between these surfaces, there is always an imperceptible distance of air; however, in the case of touch there is the absolutely simultaneous experience of the medium and the experience of what arrives through the medium.[28] Thus, physical immediacy and phenomenological immediacy are in this instance at one. If we were only at the surface of *sarx,* then the experience of saturating

26. Ibid., 419a 13–15.
27. Ibid., 419a 8–419b 3.
28. Ibid., 423b 13–18: "But there is a difference between tangible things, and visible or audible things. We perceive the latter because some medium acts on us, but we perceive tangible things not by a medium, but at the same time as the medium, like a man wounded through his shield; for it is not the stricken shield that struck him, but both he and the shield were struck simultaneously."

blinding would ensue; yet we are at no physical distance whatsoever. The distance is therefore a spiritual one, the distance of folded and reflexive removal of *sarx* from itself, of *eidos* from itself as dense *hyle*, to become more fully *eidos* in luminous transparency.

Touch, the lowest mode of sensibility, most common to all souls—vegetative, animal, and intellectual—therefore *proves* the soul's peculiar instance; its removal, which is even, for Aristotle, in the case of the highest intellectual removal, its clear immortality. We are, as humans, immortal because we are *more* embodied—that is to say, as touching more comprehensively and with more intensity. For Aristotle says that human bodies are distinguished by greater keenness of touch, which is the *lowest* faculty; whereas in the higher sensitive capacities they must yield preeminence to other animal species. Moreover, people with more sensitive bodies are also the ones who are more intellectually able.

This circumstance is doubly bizarre, in that the intellect is immortal, and not overwhelmed by too much reason, as sight is over-whelmed and destroyed as sight by a dazzling light, or hearing by a deafening sound.[29] Yet touch is not only destroyable as touch: Too harsh a touch can kill the whole organism.[30] Touch, therefore, is the existential faculty; it mediates our being towards death. Yet as such, it also permits the exercise of the immortal and indestructible faculty. Opposites remarkably coincide here, since the exercise of the invulnerable only emerges through the attempt to secure a relative security, whose precondition is nevertheless exposure to danger. For in sensing danger, we render ourselves open to being sensed in turn, on the basis of the general principle that the sensing must also be one among the objects sensed. Therefore, if touch proves the soul, our inhabitation of animal life unto death also proves our immortal life. *Because* we die, we live. Or more exactly, because we can die a

---

29.   Ibid., 426a 27–426b 69; 429b–429b 6: "[N]either seeing nor smelling is possible just after strong colours and scent; but when mind thinks the highly in intelligible, it is not less able to think of slighter things, but even more able."

30.   Ibid., 435b 4–26.

specifically *human* death, we live. In Christian terms, this would be the natural presence of resurrection everywhere, despite our fall-induced death, exposed by the resurrection of Christ.

Since touch is mediated by the flesh, there is also a distance, a transparency involved in touch, as much as with vision. But this is now much more emphatically an inner-reflected, psychic transparency. Inversely, however, Aristotle declares that *all* sensation involves the immediacy of touch, since even the transparencies of light and air are mediated by a series of contiguous bodies.[31] And through the transparent medium of light, the eye really does touch the visible object. Therefore, all sensation is touching and occurs only by the medium of the flesh. Therefore again, the visible medium collapsed as touch into immediacy regains mediation as the inner psychic distance.

Merleau-Ponty also affirmed that touch is mediated vision, and vision is mediated touch. He regarded this as yet another instance of reciprocal intertwining—noting that all touching falls within the field of the visible, while all that is seen is what can potentially be touched.

So far, it has been seen that sensation arises in connection with the needs of the self-moving—that is, organisms—for survival and increase. However, the perspective of both Aristotle and Merleau-Ponty, which pivots round the sequence of formed flesh that is "prior" to both matter and spirit, suggests that there can be no functional reductivism involved here. If sensation is for motion, then equally motion is for sensation, since this is always at a psychic distance, and therefore can always aesthetically remove itself from its pragmatic origins. And if the sensed can only be grasped as teleologically *for* sensation, then all beings share in this contemplative destiny.

It follows that we can equally grasp motion as *for* sensation: These two realities also move in reciprocal, intertwined circles. Merleau-Ponty observes that in order to sense we must also move: We must travel to the right vantage point then swivel or focus our eyes; we must move and control our hands in order to feel, brushing gently if we wish to register a subtle texture. Just as we ourselves must

---

31. Ibid., 435a 9–20.

be visible in order to see, so in order to register mobile realities, we must not only be ourselves capable of motion, but must even actually move amid these realities. It is not the case that vision is ideally possible from a fixed best perspective; instead, vision would not be possible at all if there *was* such a perspective. Rather, vision is possible as an exchange of gazes, in which realities are only ever shown to a point of view as themselves points of view. Merleau-Ponty rightly interpreted Renaissance perspective as this realization and not as a new assertion of objectivity.[32]

In Aristotelian terms, the flesh is not only the site of sound, senses, vision, and touch in double (objective and subjective) senses, it is also the site of *appetite,* which equally moves and is moved, and as such forms the cusp between body and soul, just as a ball-joint fits into its bearing.[33] Appetite, as involved in motion, does not, for Aristotle, belong to the soul proper, or rather not to the higher imaginative and reasoning soul. This doctrine of an apathetic *psyche* can seem unsympathetically spiritualizing, but the point is that for Aristotle it is the entire hylomorphic entity that feels, not the soul as such. Thus, he points out that we do not say "the soul gets angry," any more than we say "the soul weaves or builds a house."[34] Instead, the soul is either the terminus or the origin of movement: In perception, movement starts from particular objects and ends in the soul; in recollection, the impulse begins in the soul and extends to movement in the sense organ.[35] In both cases, the soul does not retreat from activity, but rather perfects it, since transitional movement (*kinesis*) is only on its way from potency to activity, whereas the soul as *entelechia* is perfectly realized *energeia*, whose effectiveness is self-realizing and therefore beyond alteration. Nevertheless, the highest level of the soul

---

32. Maurice Merleau-Ponty, "Working Notes," in *The Visible and the Invisible* (Evanston, Ill.: Northwestern University Press, 1973), 212. See also, James Elkin, *The Poetics of Perspective* (Ithaca, N.Y.: Cornell University Press, 1994). I am indebted to Conor Cunningham for calling my attention to this book and its topic.

33. Aristotle, *De Anima,* 433b 21–23.

34. Ibid., 408b 11–17.

35. Ibid., 408b 11–18.

possesses its own active appetition that is *boulesis*.[36] As we shall see in the next section, this appetition always accompanies intellection, and hence, it does not appear to be true, at least in the *De Anima,* that there is nothing at all like "will" in Aristotle: There is indeed no modern, uninflected neutral will, but then that is also absent in Christian writers like Augustine. In this text, *boulesis* as higher appetition seems not unlike the Platonic *eros*.[37]

It is flesh as appetite that always registers sensations according to pleasure or aversion. In fact, all that is ever registered is a beautiful proportion or its lack. In the case of hearing, what one hears in hearing sound is sound *as* the proportion between sound sounded and sound heard: There is no merely objective sound to be heard that is not orientated toward hearing. This is why sound is, as such, harmony: Sounds are normally pleasant, and an unpleasant sound will grate. There never are heard any merely neutral sounds, outside harmony or its lack, and so not in some measure pleasing or unpleasing. Indeed, as we have already intimated, an extreme of disharmony actually removes the capacity for hearing, so showing, negatively, that it is, literally, sound that makes itself heard. In this way it communicates both *dynamis* and *logos*.[38] Even more fundamentally, touch is to

---

36.   Ibid., 432b 5–8; 433a 23–25.

37.   For a good statement of the view that there is no such thing as the "will" in Aristotle, see J-P Vernant, "Intimidations of the Will in Greek Tragedy," in J-P Vernant and P. Vidal-Nacquet, *Myth and Tragedy in Ancient Greece* (New York: Zone, 1990), 49–85. Vernant argues mostly from the Nicomachean Ethics and accuses Aristotle of a "confusion" between "the internal, the spontaneous, and what is really autonomous." But does not this verdict reflect the Cartesian bias of the French tradition of historiography of Greek judicial concepts from Louis Gernet onward? A story is always told of an "'evolution" toward the discrimination of faculties and of the will that seems to presuppose a Cartesian (and Kantian) account of "a pure choosing will" distinct from desire, affection, and an inclination infused by reason. Yet such a concept of will is not self-evident—before Descartes, its stoic, semi-pelagian, Abelardian, Scotist, and nominalist adumbrations were always rigorously countered by Maximian, Augustinian, and Thomist traditions.

38.   Aristotle, *De Anima,* 424a 28.

do with aesthetic harmony. Thus the most acute touch is literally and metaphorically "taste." Aristotle says that "touch is a kind of mean between all tangible qualities."[39] Unlike the qualities known to the other senses, those known to touch are diverse: hot and cold, rough and smooth, and so forth. Touch can register and mediate them all, because the body is itself composed of all the diverse elements in due proportion.

Likewise, Merleau-Ponty speaks of a "'participation" and a "kinship" between objective and subjective sound, light, and touch. Between these two halves of a never quite foreclosed circle, there is, he declares, a "reciprocity" and a "tangling."

Normally, for the tradition, including Aristotle, hearing and especially vision are more allied to incorporeal intellect that is the sense of touch. But in *De Anima,* Aristotle envisages a strange sort of psychic kenosis, where the soul occurs within a self-emptying toward the precariousness of existence. It is also therein affirmed, as we have seen, that touch is the most generic of the senses, the nearest to showing sense as such. One would go wrong in supposing this to be an "empirical" modification to the Platonic preference for vision. For, to the contrary, it is the tactile proof of the soul that demands, for Aristotle, that real vision, the real mediated transparent distance, always be a psychic distance opened up in the fold of flesh itself.

Inversely, Merleau-Ponty's new phenomenological insistence upon touch, while it equally does not displace vision, ensures it cannot be merely eidetic vision of appearances within an immanent space, as for Husserl. Instead, it must be vision of real material things in themselves. But the relative switch from vision to touch does also disturb the sway of phenomenology as such. It is true that, within this philosophy, vision is meant as a metaphor for all manifestation, assuming no privilege for eyesight. However, such a privileging does seem to intrude when appearing is thought of (as by Husserl, and even in the end as we have seen, Heidegger, Derrida, and Levinas) on the model of objects as shown before a neutral uninflected subject. (Marion escapes this only by recourse to voluntarism.) By contrast,

---

39. Ibid., 435a 22–24; 423b 26–424a 16.

where thought is construed as founded upon touch, then attention to appearance has to share priority with ineradicable feeling, since touch always feels harmony (kinship, participation) or its lack; and also with construction, since the hand that touches can only touch in molding and transforming. If it is true that the hand may only touch as subject because it is also an object that may be touched, then it is also true that the touched object can only affect us because we can affect it, and potentially, much more powerfully and more purposefully. This is presumably why Merleau-Ponty says that the body is the *exemplary* sensible. Therefore, Merleau-Ponty, unlike other phenomenologists, gives equal parity to feeling and construction along with eidetic intuition in his construal of the nature of thought. That he likewise gives equal parity to conjecture, we shall see in the next section.

THE ENTANGLED PSYCHE

We have seen how the sensed folds back upon itself into sensation. In the second place, sensation folds back upon itself into intellection, for both Aristotle and Merleau-Ponty.

Aristotle's figure of the fold is actually an unfolding. The "bent line" of sensed flesh "straightens itself out" as *sensus communis*.[40] If touch proves the soul, then, as with Plato (in the *Phaedo*), the mediation of heterogenous senses also proves the soul.[41] For this mediation is not physical and manifest; it is rather invisible and mysterious. How do we touch, see, or hear the same thing? (Kant considers the problem again in his own fashion as that of "transcendental deduction," as we have seen.) For both Plato and Aristotle there must be a psychic "common sense" that grasps a hidden proportion between the incommensurable. As connected by common sense, the various sensing faculties are, for Aristotle, "numerically and analogically one," according to an analogy of comparable ratios (Aquinas will later move

---

40.   Ibid., 429b 16–21.
41.   Ibid., 425a 14–425b 12; 426b 8–24.

beyond this toward a more purely ineffable kinship and *convenientia*).[42]

Common sense involves imagination, which is a relative abstraction of *eide* from *hyle*. But if this abstraction and mediation is possible, then presumably it is because of the function of mediation and abstraction already performed by touch, which, is a common factor involved in all sensation, just as the immediacy of touch is also inhabited by the distance of vision and hearing. Common sense is, therefore, for Aristotle already latent in sensing itself, albeit as the bent line that demands (of itself) a straightening out.

Imagination is the medium in which the *judgment* of the higher soul swims. "The soul never thinks without a mental image," and the film of images is to the mind as the air is to the eye, in affecting it.[43] It is the judgment, however, and not sensory perception, nor mental imagination, that is true or false. Indeed, the mind cannot go wrong in what it perceives and imagines, insofar as it always correctly perceives or imagines *essences*; however, the perception and the imagination can mislead the judgment, insofar as they may register a misleading appearance of the *combination* of essences.[44] Here the judgment must assess the circumstances, and the ratio of what appears to what does not appear. In this way something like "conjecture" starts to impinge.

However, in the *De Anima*, judgment as conjecturing does not at all leave the feeling of sensation behind. Instead, conjecture turns out to be only the folding back upon itself, or in Aristotle's terms, the unfolding, of feeling. This happens in the following way.

As Kant later realized, the whole issue of identifying a relatively coherent object, of picking something out from the flux, or of distinguishing the *something,* depends upon the question of *time*. Aristotle realized this also. For if it is the judgment of combinations of essence that can be false as well as true, then, he observes, combinations

---

42. See Gilbert Narcisse, *Les Raisons de Dieu* (Fribourg, Switzerland: Editions Fribourg Suisse, 1997), passim.

43. Aristotle, *De Anima,* 431a 17–20; 431b 2–7; 432a 11–14.

44. Ibid., 430b 28–32; 428a 12–13.

depend upon time, and so, too, do judgments, which occur in time. They are both contingent events. However, time is aporetic. Aristotle declares that a thought takes time, and yet one cannot divide an integral thought into two halves of time, such as to say what was thought in each half. Yet time *is* in principle divisible—so any time taken by a thought ought to be divisible

This aporia becomes more acute when we think about thought as judgment. A judgment of opposite successive qualities, like bitter and sweet, seems to divide the judgment into different successive moments. Yet for judgment to work, it must be single—and therefore must occur in a "now" that holds ecstatically together the past, present, and future. Here, indeed, it is possible that Aristotle is invoking *and* endorsing Plato's oral teaching (which he has earlier described in this text), according to which the soul embraces the "oneness" of mind and the "twoness" of knowledge.[45]

A parallel aporia, according to Aristotle, arises in relation to *qualities*. The thought of a quality is likewise properly indivisible, and yet the mind can assay the division of such a thought, at least as a kind of algebraic abstraction.[46] However, both sets of divisions, of the enduring instant that does and does not take time, and of the experienced quality which is single and yet divisible as continuous, are considered by Aristotle (where it is the case that such dividing refuses the synthesis of the "two" in the "one") to be *privations,* which, when enacted by the mind, cause the mind likewise to undergo privation.[47] But the thought of a quality is itself in time. Thus, when the entire quality of a thing is misapprehended, when it is thought in terms of a false combination of essences, then, says Aristotle, it has been sundered from its own integrity. To think a wrong combination is to think a lack of quality; moreover, it is equally to think a lack in the integral event—it is to shatter the integral "now" of the event which fuses past, present, and future (and so folds out of the time series, but as the time series) into a sequence of isolated "nows" that bear

---

45.   Ibid., 404b 19–28; 426b 25–427a 15; 430b 7–430b 32.
46.   Ibid., 430b 15–30.
47.   Ibid.

the correctly intuited essences withheld from their true instance of qualitative combination. On this reading, Aristotle is even nearer to Heidegger's insights than the latter acknowledged.

But just what is the intellect judging? Primarily, it is judging sets of combinations that are presented to it by the imagination. However, its relation to these images is not first and foremost theoretical. The struggle between reason and desire is not, to begin with, one between disinterest and interest, as it would be for Kant. Rather, this struggle arises again because of time: It is the struggle between long- and short-term interest.[48] And this renders reason more like a drawn out, distanced sort of desiring. More emphatically still, the judging soul first asserts or denies images, not as true or false, but rather as good or bad. It then pursues the good and avoids the bad.[49] So this is initially the more cunning deployment of movement and sensation by a mobile and more richly sensitive animal (hairless, with a soft, sensitive surface). However, as we have already seen, this seeming functionalism in Aristotle is always exactly reversible: The soul is "the true place of forms,"[50] and if, for example, snub-nosedness occurs only in matter, nonetheless the essence or *eidos* of snubness takes off incorporeally from any particular matter, such that its precise nature, *its indeed deeper reality*, resides more properly in abstraction within the soul.[51] (Psychic functionalism in Descartes is not equivalently reversible, since for him passions do not disclose *eide*.) Thus, if our knowledge of good and bad is rooted in pleasure and pain, then nevertheless "to feel pleasure or pain is to adopt an attitude with the sensitive mean towards the good or bad as such."[52] Pleasure and pain subserve survival and increase, and yet beyond these they register irreducible harmonies, by an act of artificial abstraction from ineluctably given reality, from the only world we can really inhabit and talk about. The most immediate aspect of pleasure and pain, which is the

---

48. Ibid., 433a 22–433b 13.
49. Ibid., 431b 18–22.
50. Ibid., 429a 27–30.
51. Ibid., 429b 18–22.
52. Ibid., 431a 9–13.

unfolding of objective harmony or its lack, is nonetheless the most abstractable, that which most comes to inhabit the formal distance of *psyche*.

In this way, if the good is eudaemonistic, always a matter of pleasure, it is equally and reciprocally true that pleasure is always a matter of encountering the objectively good—the "ethical" good. This is what we first sense, and then, at a deeper level of abstraction, imagine. Only with a further act of abstraction does this good unfold still further into the "true" of the judgment. However, it is the good that retains priority and initiative. Aristotle declares that "what does not involve action, i.e., the true or the false, belongs to the same sphere as what is good or evil; but they differ in having respectively a particular and a universal reference."[53] After this statement, he goes on to illustrate what he means by "universal reference" in terms of the abstracted essence of snubness and numbers thought of without matter. However, the Aristotelian aporia of substance ensues that, while in a sense snubness is more really in the soul, in another sense it makes no sense without reference to real noses. Only the doctrine of Creation finally resolves this aporia by allowing the being of "matter" also fully to proceed from mind.[54] Therefore, if snubness is not really separable from matter, the true and the false of judgment are not really separable from the good and evil of imagination. So in this text, if not in others, Aristotle follows Plato in not dividing theoretical from practical reason; moreover, it would seem to follow that if there are good and bad things as well as notions, so also there can be true and false things as well as notions—again, as for Plato.[55]

This means that all reason is still feeling and only distinguished as a feeling for the more universal and the more elevated. As feeling,

---

53. Ibid., 431b 10–12.

54. See Edward Booth's magnificent work, *Aristotelian Apoeretic Ontology in Islamic and Christian Thinkers* (Cambridge: Cambridge University Press, 1983).

55. This would mean that, for Aristotle as well as Plato, dialectics is finally subordinated to the enticement of the Good, rendering them both more the anticipators of Augustine than I allowed in *Theology and Social Theory* (Oxford: Blackwell, 1991), chapters 11 and 12.

reason feels both the presence of the good and its lack. True and false that sustain dialectic are therefore, for Aristotle (here at least), subordinate to a feeling for the good and lack of its instance. What is false is not a sheer abyssal mistake but always a partial truth. Moreover, it can only ever appear as the less desirable. The soul is "all existing things,"[56] the "place of forms," because subjective knowledge is the objective knowable, and this in turn, as the imagination of sensation, *is* unfolded sensation, which finally is the sensible. Therefore, the soul is the felt sensible that is flesh, unfolded.

If judgment nonetheless unfolds feeling beyond feeling, this must have to do with speculation. What does not appear is also somehow seen and felt, but seen and felt only through conjecture.

Here Merleau-Ponty supplements Aristotle, with a more "postmodern" sense of absence, construction, and the mediation of signs. Aristotle does, indeed, speak of how what we see and feel are signs, such as a flashing beacon, which warns us of danger.[57] However, Merleau-Ponty has a stronger sense of absence and signification.[58] He insists that, since the cube only ever appears to us in some of its facets, and yet does appear as a distinguishable cube, that somehow the invisible sides are shown to us. Without seeing the invisible, there could be no manifest visibility, only a blinding and inchoate flux. This is not Marion's sublime appearance of the invisible in the extreme yet typical instance as saturated phenomenon, but rather an appearing of the invisible in the everyday instance, whereby it does not dazzle, but exhibits itself as a specific and beautiful form. The invisibility of the cube is shown as the nonetheless formed and appearing cube. Here, however, phenomenology is itself crossed by semiotics. For the visible sides appear as the signs of the invisible. These signs move us and convey their own verdict; yet in constituting our subjectivity, they do not really obliterate it, since the passage from the signifier to the signified is here one of judgment, and only aleatory if, indeed, the mere will of the subject intervenes. The

---

56. *De Anima,* 431b 20–22.
57. Ibid., 431b 3–7.
58. Merleau-Ponty, *The Visible and the Invisible,* passim.

passage is mediated as a certain *style,* according to Merleau-Ponty. Thus, while language "covers" the entire visible world, visibility reciprocally intrudes as the invisible "feeling" of meaning that pervades syntax and alone sustains it. In this way, semiotics is equally crossed by phenomenology. We hold onto particular phrases in music; they haunt our memory, not because of their structure, but because of their ineffable "soul," which is only possible through structure, and yet "takes off" from structure. We know that it takes off, because we can analogously convey the same or a kindred style in different and heterogenous structures.

Hence, for Merleau-Ponty, it is style that mediates the visible and the invisible. The world holds together only as a work of art, and without this recognition there could be no truth. Since the sensed is destined for, is in a way already sensing, we only see the world because it equally gazes back upon us, in tangled reciprocity.[59] This is "intercorporeity," which is founded, one can add, upon interobjectivity within the veil of flesh. Intersubjectivity builds upon this base; for given that sensation is always a fold in the sensed, we do not recognize another subject by projection of our own ego, but rather as a more intense gaze back upon us that itself further enables our own gaze, and does not simply reduce me in turn to an object. Another subject sees me as a gazer who, by the *movement* of my gaze and the construction of a new perspective, makes an active difference to the world the other is looking at. I see the other as looking at me as such a one, such a phenomenon. I know myself more as an active gazer and more operate as such. In "Interrogation and Dialectic," Merleau-Ponty refused the Levinasian and Sartrean idea of encountering the other as invisible negation, since this reduces the other to an abstract and general "for itself." Instead, he insisted that I encounter the other in his very invisibility and asymmetry in "one sole image in which we are both involved"[60] along the one visible surface of being. There is

---

59. Unlike Marion and Derrida, Merleau-Ponty (along with Sartre) seems to have received enthusiastically the Maussian paradigm of gift-exchange. See Dermot Moran, *Introduction to Phenomenology,* 443.

60. Merleau-Ponty, *The Visible and Invisible,* 89.

here a mutually enabling exchange of active interventions. In consequence, says Merleau-Ponty in "The Intertwining," when two people gaze at a landscape, one can really give his green to the other; truly, one can see another's green. To see green is not (as Wittgenstein would agree) to be locked within inviolable interiority, it is rather to move around green, re-envisage green, and give green back to green as a somewhat other green. So we can also show it to the other. To see is already to paint, and my pictures are in principle available to other people.

Aristotle almost concurred. If, for him, to know is passively to become all things, it is also actively to make (*panta poein*) all things, in the way that light produces colors.[61] For activity is first *energeia,* not *kinesis,* and activity is ontologically prior to potential. Passive reception must really be active reception, as what is received becomes actively more its true self. In Platonic tradition, however, there is less misleading sense of there being first a passive and then an active moment, and more of an idea of a single active reception.[62] And then the "making" performed by the mind runs less risk than with Aristotle's conception of evolving into an idealist *a priori* making and can be seen more as the simultaneous acting back upon real received things in the mode of physical artistic shaping and the formation of words and signs. Likewise, there is less risk of an idealist construal of the Socratic view that the soul is not properly taught but is itself the site of universals. Aristotle repeats this nostrum in the *De Anima,* but without some sense of recollection, it seems that the universals just immanently unfold from within mind as if, indeed, all lay pre-given within the soul, in contradiction of Aristotle's priority of actuality.[63] By contrast the "recall" of something transcendent to mind more requires the encounter with external things through mind, and their re-shaping by the *Logos* operating through us—since these processes

---

61. *De Anima,* 430a 22–417b 27.

62. See Pickstock, "Music: Soul, City and Cosmos." in *Radical Orthodoxy* (ed. J. Milbank, C. Pickstock, G. Ward; London: Routledge, 1999), 243–77.

63. *De Anima,* 417a 22–417b 27.

alone trigger recollection. In this way, by adding recollection to tele-
ology, the immortal soul that is paradoxically unfolded flesh is yet
more firmly folded back into flesh, if it is to be true to its immortal
essence, and after death, gain itself forever.

INTIMATIONS OF IMMORTALITY

Yet for Merleau-Ponty, the soul is not immortal. Can one think of
the soul of beautiful reciprocity without God, within immanence?

Merleau-Ponty carries out the reduction to pure intuited givenness beyond such givenness, to reach a pre-reflexive level (yet folded
back upon relexivity), wherein appearance is crossed by judging conjecture and linguistic construction, and appearance itself is as much
felt as seen, and so given only in a specific mood. Unlike Heidegger,
Derrida, Levinas, and Marion, however, Merleau-Ponty seems to sustain this interruption of phenomenology at the highest transcendental level. No synthesis ever takes place between the asymmetrically
disposed circles, and no pure objective account is offered concerning
the entire situation in which body interlocks with world. Indeed, one
could read Merleau-Ponty as finally reviving Brentano's original psychologism that haunted phenomenology from the outset, and which
was always linked to the *De Anima,* and not only to J. S. Mill's
empiricist reduction of logic to mere contingent biology. For if the
soul participates in the immortal mind, then the insistence that logic
is psychic is no empiricistic denigration of the objectivity of logic.[64]

---

64. See Martin Kusch, *Psychologism* (London: Routledge, 1997), and
Dermont Moran, *Introduction,* 23–59. Kusch's superb and iconoclastic
book, which suggests the limitations of (nearly) *all* twentieth-century philosophy, nonetheless may underrate the nineteenth-century Roman Catholic
prehistory of psychologism versus intuitionism in the conflicts between
Aristotlians/Thomists and Malebranchsian ontologists and correlatively fails
to see that while the end of "anti-psychologism" (*both* analytic and phenomenological philosophy), might issue in a renewed naturalism, it could equally
allow the return of a metaphysics orientated toward transcendence. For
what this ending renders dubious is not traditional realist metaphysics, but

In this respect, Merleau-Ponty veers more toward a kind of Protagorean relativism.[65] He identifies flesh with ontological Being, and the transactions within flesh with ontic events. However, the relation between them is not conceived in terms of the hypostatization of flesh as an appearing inapparent, or sublimity: This is impossible, given that flesh is the receding horizon of a nonetheless specific surface. Nor is it conceived in terms of the disguising of flesh in the event of appearing, through which disguising, flesh is all the same fated to be flesh. There is no Germanic pagan-gnostic drama of fated fallenness at work here. Instead, the Latinizing of Heidegger allows that flesh is reliably and truly disclosed within perception. All the moments of "style" that are received and constituted give the very being of flesh itself. One trusts, and has faith in, the perceived beauty of the world as the beauty of Being as such. Likewise, the crossing of regards in Merleau-Ponty is not simply the meeting of essentially one-way and sublime gazes upon sublimity, as for Marion. Instead, a specific content and style is constituted in this crossing, which is thereby a circulation as much as an intersection.

But does such an account do justice to the reality of *time?* In *The Phenomenology of Perception,* Merleau-Ponty took over from Husserl and Heidegger the view that we do not constitute time, but rather are constituted by the tangled inter-involvement of past, present, and future.[66] Nevertheless, Merleau-Ponty considered here that time belongs entirely to *our* mode of being. In the world as such, past, present, and future are all co-present in a kind of spatial simultaneity—although for Merleau-Ponty, space itself does not involve discrete

---

all philosophies that imagine a stable immanent universe of eternal (but not transcendent) logical entities, or given structures of eidetic intuition, and so on. Kusch also very oddly supposes that explanation in terms of social context is somehow intrinsically allied to naturalism, whereas of course it is ontologically neutral and could be used equally to cast relativistic cultural suspicion upon naturalistic positions.

65. See Moran, *Introduction to Phenomenology,* 391–434.

66. Maurice Merleau-Ponty, *The Phenomenology of Perception* (trans. Colin Smith; London: Routledge, 1991), 410–34.

points, any more than time involves discrete nows. Only the subjective mover across space introduces absence into plenitude, as he
retains the places he leaves, cannot quite grasp the place he is now in
(as too close to him in its nowness), and anticipates the place he is yet
to arrive at. When Merleau-Ponty later switches to a more ontological perspective, his views on time are less clear, because they are left to
us in sketchy form. In a notebook entry he rejects both viewing time
"from above," as if it was already there (his earlier view, in some
ways?), and the idea that a supplementary now could keep arriving
from the future, pushing the whole series of foregoing nows into the
past. This seems to amount to a refusal of a Heideggerean primacy of
flux, as relying on an active nothingness—the future nothing arriving
as something. Instead, Merleau-Ponty obscurely says that the new
present is something both there and not there, and "is a cycle defined
by a central and dominant region with indecisive contours."[67] So
even if time is now no longer within the subject, it still seems to be
subordinated to spatial circularity.

Can such a view make sense? Merleau-Ponty has an important
point, as against postmodernism. For time is not necessarily an irreversible one-way arrow. If time is ecstatic, not a succession of discrete
nows, then it is only sheerly linear for a particular coding. How do
we know that past moments do not in some sense return, as if time
obeyed an absolute Newtonian calendar without days, weeks, months,
and years?[68] For Augustine, and Bede in his wake, this was certainly
not the case, since they discerned a great cosmic week ending in an
eschatological sabbath, as well as the recurring one composed of the
sun's daily cycles. Merleau-Ponty rightly insists in *The Phenomenology
of Perception,* against Heidegger, that we can never exit from the sup-
posedly unauthentic now-time of the instance into a purely ecstatic
being that expresses fully the reality of flux.[69] For Merleau-Ponty this

67. Merleau-Ponty, "Working Notes," in *The Visible and the Invisible,*
184–85, 190–92, 194–95.
68. Catherine Pickstock pointed this out to me about nine years ago.
69. *Phenomenology of Perception,* 410–34.

is not really a resignation to ontic fallenness, since the ecstasy runs in an ever-renewed cycle in which the simultaneous hiding and revealing of time and presence in the now itself conveys a harmonious rhythm, and not a tragic loss that we must impossibly seek to undo. However, against Merleau-Ponty one must point out that time *is* the time of unprecedented arrival and of irreversible one-way gift. Things occur, never to return. Yes, one can conjecture that their loss is also their later returning as different, since they are given as self-differentiating and so as living. But this suggests a spiraling and not a pure circling. In this way, the arrow and the cycle can be integrated.

Merleau-Ponty's later vision of space also suggests a spiraling, and so seems to require time as its co-ordinate. However, his reluctance to think of arrival from an absolutely null future means that all the reality of flesh must lapse back into an eternal presence of circularity. His is an immanence of spatial plenitude, not of absent/present fluctuation. It is an immanence anxious to refuse nihilism—and so in spirit, utterly commendable.

But is it coherent? Normally immanence issues (paradoxically) in a perspectival dualism, as in the case of Spinoza (substance and modes). If the absolute is within finite reality, then there is a secret, eternal presence of this reality that is only disguised in the modes of times. These modes do not participate in, do not analogically disclose, the hidden absolute. Yet Merleau-Ponty speaks as if the absolute of flesh is faithfully conveyed in the beauty of all perception. His model is not pantheism, but rather, as he clearly confesses, a decapitated Catholic theology in which God incarnate is *only* incarnate and incarnate everywhere. So just as Thomas Aquinas saw the *esse* of the God-Man as identical with the divine *esse,* so Merleau-Ponty sees the ontological on the surface everywhere, immediately and fully present to the ontic.[70]

Yet *can* this work? The decapitated Incarnation is pantheism all the same. A recognized transcendence would have allowed Merleau-Ponty to admit absolute arrival from the future without lapsing into

---

70.   See Maurice Merleau-Ponty, "Faith and Good Faith," in *Sense and Non-Sense* (trans. H. L. and P. H. Dreyfus; Evanston, Ill.: Northwestern University Press 1964), 172–82.

Heidegger's nihilism. Instead, if spatial plenitude finally reigns, then all the temporal events of perceiving, all embodiments, must after all belong to a lesser level of mere appearing, which disguises simultaneity. Unique arriving events of style and kinship resolve back into a specifically named "pre-established harmony" between the two halves of the *chiasmus*.[71] Each true glance must after all transport us beyond event into an earthly paradisal bliss that is always there, and always the same. Sartre noted that Merleau-Ponty never recovered from a blissful childhood on the western coast of France.[72] Of course, such visions were sometimes enjoyed by Patristic sages, but only within a horizon that also allowed for the restoration of fallen passing moments. Spatial immanence rather implies that passing moments are exited from by the soul and that their fallenness need not be remedied.

Despite his unrivaled evocation of reciprocity, Merleau-Ponty finally speaks of *narcissism*. To be fair, this is not merely me seeing myself in reflection, but rather my seeing myself *only* in reflection.[73] The Narcissus is not I, nor the other, but rather the entire circle of flesh itself. Thus, Merleau-Ponty speaks of two mirrors forever exchanging contents that *are* only in the other mirror. Yet the nihilistic abyss seems to open up after all, if the circularity is of an immanent One, who only *is* through its two never-synthesized aspects. In that case all it is, as the ultimate, is the empty mutuality of ceaseless echo. At this level there is indeed only a single circle and no gift.

Whereas if there is to be ultimate gift, then a spiraling must preserve both space and time in co-primacy. There must be both exchange *and* loss of the gift, if one is to have an asymmetrical reciprocity and a non-identical repetition. Here Marion's exactly half-correct perspective itself returns to supplement and be in turn supplemented by that of Merleau-Ponty. The reciprocating circles of twin souls must not be

---

71. Merleau-Ponty, "The Intertwining," 133.
72. Moran, *Introduction to Phenomenology*, 391.
73. "The Intertwining," 139–41; "Working Notes," 155–56 (in the latter passage, narcissism sounds more like narcissism plain and simple—but this is but a jotting).

superseded by one impersonal circle, but must be given themselves, in their twin, never-interlocking circularity, by an elevated otherness. If, all the same, the gift they are offered is not merely the empty gift of one-way sacrifice, but rather the gift *of* reciprocity, then what is disclosed is transcendent otherness that is itself personal exchange: eternal spiraling, not an eternal and impersonal unity. Incarnation may not, after all, sustain incarnation without the drama of the Trinity—within whose immanence the reciprocating two are again preserved from mutual narcissism by the grant of a third instance that is active as well as receptive *donum*.

Nor, then, may the reciprocal soul reciprocate, unless it be immortal: given from, in order to return to, an eternal existence. But this implies equally the deified destiny of the flesh, of which the soul is the unfolded form. For if Aristotle, as we saw, divined the resurrection of the soul, then it was left to Christianity to glimpse the immortality of the body.[74] In the combination of both lies our final share in beauty.

---

74. Catherine Pickstock has pointed out a similar dimension of "Resurrection" in Plato's *Phaedo,* in her *A Short Guide to Plato* (Oxford: Oxford University Press, forthcoming).

2

The Beauty of God*

Graham Ward

Everything we do, we create, we imagine, we interpret, and we compose is implicated in complex cultural operations, multifarious social dynamics. We can never rise above nor erase the historical and cultural conditions we inhabit. That does not mean there is only one culture at any one time. There are trends, counter-trends, and radical alternatives criss-crossing through every epoch and its dominant fashions that pluralize culture. Being implicated in complex cultural politics does not mean everything can be reduced to, because it is fully determined by, a particular culture. There are always other influences, hybrid, creative syntheses unaccountable by cultural mores. But being implicated in complex cultural operations does mean that the aesthetic activity that gains value in any culture is inseparable from the way that culture both understands important aesthetic categories like form, beauty, color, texture, composition, and understands the act of representation. We are, after all, *taught* how to paint to compose, to sculpt, to write, to interpret, and to appreciate. There is a training,

---

*   I would like to thank Walter Lowe and James K. A. Smith for their important remarks upon and criticisms of earlier drafts of this essay.

an education—even if that training is later rejected. What we judge and produce as beautiful is profoundly related to what we understand Beauty to be. If a world rejects, and lives out the rejection, of transcendental values, or if a world lives in the wake of the death of God and what I will term the "opacity of creation," then what it produces and what it passes on to be internalized is a view of the aesthetic that is secularized. To put this in terms of the theology of icons—to which I will return—to deny the possibility of the sanctification and deification of human nature, to deny the participation of creation in the uncreated God, is to conceive the world as opaque, inert data. Such a denial alters the very possibilities not only for the conception of the beautiful, but the representation or re-presentation of Beauty. I have not the space to pursue that secularization of the beautiful, but I wish to open a space for discussion about that secularization and its aesthetic (not to say ethical) effects. And so as I outline a Christian aesthetics that focuses on the making and veneration of icons, or what might be termed the "economy of the icon," I will allude to the figuration and appeal of the idol, the false image. Much has been made recently by the theologian and phenomenologist Jean-Luc Marion of the "conflict between two phenomenologies,"[1] that of the idol and that of the icon. In the development here of a theological phenomenology (of sorts), I will be conducting a critical conversation with Marion's post-Kantian thinking.

I want to begin with a short story, and from an exegesis of this story arrive at a Christian theological aesthetics that I hope might form the basis for a theological *Kulturkritik* of secular understandings of the beautiful. The story is told by the eighth-century theologian John Damascene as part of his apologia for icons. It concerns the making of the first icon of Christ, which, in Damascene's time, was

---

1. *God Without Being* (trans. Thomas A. Carlson; Chicago: University of Chicago Press, 1991), 7. Marion conducts a more detailed theological analysis of the idol and the icon with respect to the eighth- and ninth-century iconophiles in his essay "le Prototype et l'Image" in his volume *La Croisée du visible* (Paris: La Différence, 1991), 117–54, and more recently in *De Surcroît* (Paris: Presses Universitaires de France, 2001), 65–98, 125–53.

still on show in the city of Edessa. The icon was lost during the sack of Constantinople (where it had been taken in 944) by the Crusaders. I should point out that my analysis is more a theological reflection based upon a close reading of the text and some knowledge of the context. This is not an essay on Byzantine iconography as such. If we cannot transcend our cultural location, we cannot return to one. My visitation, then, to orthodox thinking of the Byzantine period is not an attempt to "recover" but to engage in a tradition that enables us to think otherwise. The history of the story's transmission is complex,[2] but what interests me is the way Damascene makes something of it all of his own.

> When Abgar was lord [*kurios*] of the city of
> Edessenes, he sent an artist [*zographon aposteilanti*]
> to make a portrait [*homoiographesai eikona*] of the
> Lord [*kuriou*]. When the artist was unable to do this
> because of the radiance of His face, the Lord
> Himself pressed a bit of cloth to His own sacred and
> life-giving face and left His own image on the cloth
> and so sent [*aposteilai*] this to Abgar who had
> earnestly desired it.[3]

2.   The complex history of the transmission of and changes to this story has a now developed a critical history of its own. It began with E. von Dobschutz, *Christusbilder Untersuchungen zur christlichen Legende, Texts und Untersuchungen zur Geschichte der altchristlichen Literatur,* XVIII (Leipzig:, 1899), 102–96, and continued to the present day. See Steven Runciman, "Some Remarks on the Image of Edessa," *Cambridge Historical Journal* 3 (1929–30): 238–52; Averil Cameron, "The History of the Image of Edessa: The Telling of a Story," *Harvard Ukrainian Studies* 7 (1983): 80–94; Leonid Oupensky's *Theology of the Icon,* vol. 1 (trans. Anthony Gythiel; New York: St. Vladimir's Seminary Press, 1992), 51–53; and the essays by Han J. W. Drijvers, "The Image of Edessa in the Syriac Tradition," (pp. 13–31) and Averil Cameron, "The Mandylion and Byzantine Iconclasm," (pp. 33–54) in Herbert L. Kessler and Gerhard Wolf, eds., *The Holy Face and the Paradox of Representation* (Bologna: Nouva Alfa Editoriale, 1998).

3.   De Fide Orthodoxa, in *Schriften des Johannes von Damaskos,* vol. 2 (ed. B. Kotter; Berlin: Walter de Gruyter, 1973), IV.16.51–6. English trans.

In thinking through the beauty of God, this story enables us to understand what constitutes the manifestation of that beauty. The doctrinal focus of both this story and apprehending the beauty of God is incarnation.[4] In his three tracts devoted to images, Damascene's main argument is that to reject the icon is to reject incarnation. The incarnational creativity unfolds in two stages. The first is that in which the Uncreated creator becomes a creature, a hypostasis, a person with a face. The Son was the first image of the Father, "the living image of Himself, the natural and unchangeable image of His eternity."[5] The second stage is that in which this divine human form presses His face to "the bit of cloth," leaving his own image upon it. But the doctrine of the incarnation is not all that constitutes the manifestation of the radiant beauty of Christ's face. This is the fundamental point I wish to make about a Christian aesthetics and Damascene's development of the story—that beauty is an operation, a co-operation; it is not a property but the animator of the properties of any object. To return specifically to our story: Though the beauty is ultimately that which is essential to the Lord being Lord, inseparable from his sacred and life-giving nature, the manifestation of that beauty requires and involves several others. Let's deal with the most obvious two. There is Abgar, the "lord of the city" and there is the artist. We will examine the role and operations of these characters separately in order to best approach the manner in which the beauty of God is made manifest.

Abgar is named—in Eusebius he is a king who receives a letter from Jesus that Eusebius quotes. He has a concrete place (Edessa)

F. H. Chase, *St. John of Damascus, Writings* (Washington: Catholic University of America Press, 1958), 372–73.

4.   Some have argued that the doctrinal focus of the Orthodox icon debates was Christology, but I agree with Andrew Louth that for John Damascene the incarnation is central. See Andrew Louth, *St. John Damascene: Tradition and Originality in Byzantine Theology* (Oxford: Oxford University Press, 2002), 212.

5.   Damascene, *Images III,* 26 (trans. Mary H. Allies; London: Thomas Baker, 1989). This is a development of a Pauline idea found in Col 3:10.

and a concrete position (lord of the city) in the world. The place and position are significant. The manifestation of the beauty of God is given an urban, social context—the city. It is, furthermore, given to the man who represents that city in his own person, as "lord." Abgar stands vicariously for the whole community for which he is the head. As such he stands in something of an analogical relationship to Christ Himself, as Lord. Damascene employs the word *kurios* with respect to both of them. We will return to this analogy and the question of representation it installs later. For now, let me draw attention to Abgar's action and intention. Desire is the animator of Abgar's intention.[6] Love directs the will to act and the action that follows is the "sending" of the artist. The structure of the story is the satisfaction of the desire that is its catalyst—the image of Christ is given to that person who "had so earnestly desired it." Desire, then, is one of the constitutive principles governing the manifestation of God's beauty. In Abgar's desire, he already possesses that which will enable him to recognize that the cloth given to him bears the image of a Christ he has never seen in person. Desire reaches forward toward that which it already, inchoately, possesses. It apprehends that which it cannot see and then attains an understanding of that apprehension in the delivery of what it desired. The beautiful becomes, then, a mode of re-cognition in an operation of desire.

I emphasis the "re" here in order to draw attention to the important role memory plays, not only in a theology of icons, but in theology *per se*. A theological understanding of memory, issuing from an anthropology in which salvation is the return to a knowledge of being made "in the image of" (the profound mystery of being human), is most evident in Augustine's *Confessions*. On one level, memory enables him to recall the movement of grace within his life—

6. Following Damascene, in the early ninth century, the orthodox Theodore Abu Qurrah, in his own tract "On the Practice of Venerating Images," turns the whole economy of iconic participation on the mode of intention governing both the making and the gazing. See pp. 56–61 in Sidney H. Griffith's translation "Theodore Abu Qurrah's Arabic Tract on the Practice of Venerating Images," *Journal of the American Oriental Society* 105 (1985): 53–73.

how God brought him to be baptized in and profess the Christian faith. But on another level, as in Plato, there is a relationship between memory and knowledge. What Augustine comes to know about God and about himself is that which the fallen condition of human being has caused to be forgotten or obscured: the knowledge of the God in whose image we are created. In a sense, then, all knowledge of what is good, what is true, what is beautiful, and what is just is a *re*-cognition of that image of God, that mystery of being human. As Augustine understood, the turn to what is truly most oneself is a turn to God—a God whose attributes we can recognize in the world because of the nature of our own making. Theodore Abu Qurrah explains that in the veneration of icons or the cross it is the faculty of memory that stirs the worshipper to imitation. It is not simply an account of the importance of memory as a faculty of recall but memory as an exploration of a relation between the image of God as Christ or in the lives of the saints and the venerator's life. Memory is a motor facilitating a participation in the process of redemption as *re*-cognition. Something of the circularity and temporal complexity (in which the present cogitations of memory open the self to a future state) can be heard in St. Paul's phrase "to know even as I am known" (1 Cor 13:12).

The sacred image stirs an ancient memory, a re-cognition; it *does* something, rather than simply *is* something. The beautiful is not constituted by the emotional effect upon the mind of certain properties perceived—such as harmonious proportions or a balanced turn of phrase or a certain combination of sounds rhythmically spaced. Nor does the object being perceived have any autonomy. It is not isolated like a modern work of art but part of several economies operating simultaneously: desire, production, representation, divine participation. It is in this way, and we shall develop this further, that theological aesthetics departs from psycho-philosophical aesthetics, particularly after Kant.[7]

---

7.   Marion's phenomenological account of the idolatrous gaze is founded implicitly upon the Kantian dualism of the noumenal and the phenomenal. In fact, despite his reversal of the Husserlian emphasis—

To understand the *theo* logic behind this mode of apprehension we need to appreciate a theological anthropology. Two points are axiomatic. First, to be made in God's image renders all human persons essentially ineffable. Damascene writes, "For what reason . . . do we adore one another except because we have been made in the image of God."[8] Secondly, to be made in the image of God accentuates that human beings are creative fashioners of images also. Damascene relates this understanding of what it is to be human to a theological aesthetics centered upon the incarnation of Christ: "[W]ho can make a copy [*poiesasthai mimema*] of the invisible [*aoratou*], incorporeal [*asomatou*], uncircumscribed [*aschematistou*], and unportrayable [*aperigraphtou*] God?" he asks, employing rhetorically

---

giving attention to the primary donation rather than the structures of intentionality—Marion' s phenomenology, like Husserl's, remains a product of a Kantian heritage. Hence Marion' s account of iconicity has affinities with Kant's account of the sublime and Jean-François Lyotard's explicitly Kantian aesthetics of the "unpresentable." The analysis is centered upon the rupturing event of the Cross "as the type *par excellence*" (*La Croisée du visible*, 128). Baptizing M. Merleau-Ponty's exploration of the *chiasmus,* and emphasizing a certain dialectical violence in which "the invisible is certainly not delivered in a spectacle visible to all, directly and without the mediation of a hermeneutic, but is made recognisable in [*par*] a certain visibility which it invests excessively [*surabondamment*]" (130), for Marion the Cross "manifests nothing less than the unnameable, that which had no name in any tongue" (127). A more developed and nuanced account of analogy and participation is necessary to prevent this thinking from rehearsing the dualisms that found modernity. The theological phenomenology I am developing here refuses the Kantian dualism that fosters such violences and Barthian emphases upon the ruptures of the Cross. Theologically, these emphases lead either to Docetism or Nestorianism. The theological account I wish to develop places more emphasis upon Christ and the incarnation rather than isolates one (even though decisive) moment in the *oikonomia*—the crucifixion. A theological phenomenology would also reject the subject-object negotiations that follow from the Kantian dualism and which it bequeathed to the phenomenological project.

8.   *De Fide Orthodoxa,* 370.

the Greek privative *alpha*.[9] Only God can make a copy of Godself, but human beings nevertheless are *homo symbolicus* because each is constituted as an image; each represents, incarnates, something of God. Theodore Abu Qurrah develops this idea explicitly in his "On the Practice of Venerating Images" when he asks "Is not writing only an icon for audible speech? So, this [God's writing on the tablets of the Law] is an icon for the primordial, talking Word."[10] And, further, since saints "stand as images of God,"[11] and rendering the symbolic is an aspect of being in the image of God, then "blessed be anyone who makes an icon of Christ our Lord . . . so too anyone who makes icons of his saints."[12]

We represent because we are ourselves a representation, and so to represent is not only a human action but a *divinely sanctioned* human action. Each person stands analogically related to Christ, fashioning icons of the primordial Word. But the analogical nature of that relation is fundamental, because the image, being derived, cannot represent to itself the original. Hence, Damascene's string of negative predicates: invisible, incorporeal, uncircumscribed, and unportrayable ("it is better to discuss Him by abstraction from all things"[13]). Hence also, the inability of the artist in the story to provide that for which he has been asked. Only Christ can provide an image of His own face. Only God can make a representation of God. The making is a begetting—in that the Son is the one who is begotten of the unbegotten. God's making is an extension, or procession,

---

9.   Ibid., Kotter, IV. 16.24–5; 371. Inexplicably the translation reverses "uncircumcscribed" and "unportrayable." With Theodore of Studion, who develops Damascene's Aristotelian leanings, "circumscription" becomes a major category for his thinking about icons. See Kenneth Parry, *Depicting the Word: Byzantine Iconophile Thought of the Eighth and Ninth Centuries* (Leiden: E. J. Brill, 1996), 99–113.

10.   Griffith, "Theodore Abu Qurrah's Arabic Tract," 71.

11.   Ibid., 89.

12.   Ibid., 96. For John Damascene's own theology of the image, see Andrew Louth, *St. John Damascene,* 216.

13.   Ibid., 171.

of God's self. This establishes a certain logical tension focusing on that "bit of cloth" that received the impress of Christ's face; its densely enigmatic form parallels the enigma of incarnation itself. For in Christ making an image of himself, what is produced partakes of both the human capacity to make images and the divine capacity to beget. The radiance, the beauty of Christ's face on that cloth, is an image, not the original, but it is also an operation (as distinct from, but analogous to, intratrinitarian procession). That is, there is a movement of God's self toward making manifest that all things not only belong to him, but participate in Him. "This is my face" the giving of the cloth suggests; echoing the sacramental "This is my body."[14]

Put another way, the beauty of Christ makes manifest His own watermark within creation, since by Him and through Him all things were, are, and continue to be. What is re-cognized in the beautiful, as the beautiful, is the paradisial—creation is re-cognized in terms of its Christic orientation and perfection.[15] The cloth remains cloth, is not despised as being cloth but in fact realizes its own substance in Christ (by the operation of Christ upon it). The

---

14. Kenneth Parry observes, "It was not unknown for priests to remove paint from icons to mix with the eucharistic elements, and sometimes the liturgy itself was celebrated on an icon instead of an altar," in *Depicting the Word*, 8.

15. Let us note here a significant difference with respect to Plato's reflection on the beauty and eros in *The Symposium* (ed. Kenneth Dover; Cambridge: Cambridge University Press, 1980). Diotima relates how love for the beautiful is not so much "for the beautiful itself, but for the conception and generation that the beautiful effects [*tes yenneseos kai tou tokou en to kalo*]" (*Symp.* 206 E). Damascene would concur that the manifestation of the beauty of God allows us to re-cognize the generative and creative effects of the beautiful. But because this beauty is revealed in Christ and appeals to Christ, and our desire for Christ is inseparable from Christ's desire for us, then what is loved in the beautiful *is* the beauty of God in Godself. Albeit that it is only when we see Him face to face that we will understand Him even as we have been fully understood (1 Cor 13:12).

cloth is not a vehicle.[16] Incarnation does not divide form from content or medium from message or the signifier from the signified. The beauty makes manifest something of the truth of the thing that is perfected in the manifestation—just as, even knowing all the sins X may have done by commission or omission does not prevent the priest bowing to X in adoration of the image of God within him or her. The story does not give us an account of Abgar's response to receiving the image, but the suggestion elsewhere is that the recognition of beauty calls forth praise, doxology. In the opening paragraph of his *Images III,* Damascene describes the icon as a canticle. It is part of an economy of grace that calls forth *latreia,* worship.[17] Beauty makes manifest giftedness and a participation in an eternal mystery, and it is the function of human beings in their own making to articulate that praise within creation. The records of the Seventh Ecumenical Council of 787 C.E., which deliberated on the importance of icons, state that "creation does not worship its Maker directly in its own right, but it is through me that 'the heavens declare the glory of God' (Ps 18:1), through me that the moon venerates God, through me that the stars venerate God, through me that the water, rains, dews, and the whole of creation venerate and glorify God."[18] My making participates in and testifies to God's begetting.

---

16. Damascene, *Images II*: "Although the matter is not to be worshipped in itself, if the person depicted is full of grace, it becomes a partaker of grace in proportion to faith." See also the theological realism of Gregory of Nyssa's affirmation in *On the Resurrection of the Soul*: "[C]reation indeed cries out through the things created within it and, as it were, announces its case to those able to hear inwardly that which is hymned triadically" (9).

17. In *Images III,* 104, Damascene outlines five modes of adoration. The first and highest kind is given to God alone by all created things: *latreia.* For the distinction Damascene draws between "veneration" (*proskynesis*) and "worship" (*latreia*), see Andrew Louth, *St. John Damascene,* 201.

18. Quoted in Ambrosios Giakalis, *Images of the Divine: The Theology of Icons at the Seventh Ecumenical Council* (Leiden: E. J. Brill, 1994), 123. See also Ouspensky, *Theology of the Icon,* 184–87: "Just as creation fell with the fall of man, so it is saved by the deification of man," 187.

Conceived theologically, human beings are then the priests of creation—this is fundamental to their aesthetic task. The priest is an artist. So let us turn now to the second character in what I have called the "constitution of the mode of apprehending Beauty," the beautiful as a co-operation. The artist is not the Romantic genius—the artist/priest is every person. In the story, Damascene calls the artist a portrayer of living forms [*zographon*] and associates him with a divine calling, apostleship [*aposteilanti*]. The artist is to make a portrait [*homoiographesai eikona*], not to make a copy [*poiesasthai mimema*]. In other accounts of the story, the king of Edessa sends a scribe or messenger (a *tabellarius*) who turns out to be an artist, or he sends a *tabellarius* with the instruction to bring him an icon of Christ, or he sends a number of painters to bring him an image. In what is possibly the earliest account, the one Damascene probably knew and was drawing upon (a redaction of the *Doctrina Abbai* by the fifth-century bishops of Edessa, Rabbula), the king sends Hana the archivist who then decides to paint a portrait of Jesus.[19] The idea of a God-given image may, in fact, be an interpolation into the story made as late as the 780s. So it is Damascene (who died in 749) who brings together this particular rendition of the story. It is Damascene who insists upon the role of an artist (not a scribe or archivist) who does not just reproduce; the language is much more resonant than that. The artist conveys a likeness [*homoiosis*] through the icon. The difference between likeness and image echoes Gen 1:26—"Let us make man in our image, after our likeness"—and a line of patristic reflection on *kat' eikona* and *kat'omoiosin*.[20] There is almost a sense in the language that Abgar is asking the artist to perform a task that no one can provide but God Himself, and hence immediately in the story there follows the clause "the artist was unable to do this."[21] The Greek is

---

19. See Han J. W. Drijvers and Averil Cameron in *The Holy Face and the Paradox of Representation.*

20. For example, see Clement of Alexander, *Stromateis,* n. 19.2.97 (1) (ed. Otto Stahlin; Berlin: Akademie-Verlag, 1985).

21. Damascene appears to be playing with a familiar theme of iconoclastic arguing that goes back to Eusebius of Caesarea and which Damascene himself announces: Only God can make a copy of God.

again more resonant because it repeats in a negative form the term used by Damascene for "artist": "*me dunethentos tou zographou.*" The artist may have set off believing he or she could perform this Godlike act, but the true artistic operation that issues from a proximity to Christ requires a certain surrender and re-cognition. Insofar as Christ is the "image of the Father [*eikan estin ho uios tou patros*]"[22] and also pantocrator, so human beings in their own way are made in the image of God and creators. Damascene, in his *Third Apology Against Those who Attack the Divine Images,* having distinguished six kinds of images (*eikon*), in which Christ is the first, writes: "The third kind of image is made by God as an imitation of Himself: namely man [*tritos tropos eikonos ho kata mimesin upo theo genomenos*]."[23] There is a similarity but also a difference—a difference marked by Damascene by distinguishing, at this point, icon from imitation (*mimesis*). In obeying the call to be sent, the artist learns this difference and sees Christ, himself or herself, and the world differently. In the move from Abgar to the artist we do not then move from one type of person to another, but from one mode of being in the world to another or from one mode of seeing to another.

The three characters in the narrative—Abgar, the artist, and Christ—represent the anagogical move from illumination through purification to deification. The artist is a stage in an anagogical practice of surrender. The deepening participation in creation's *latreia*[24] affords this surrender, for adoration as Damascene defines it is "a token of subjection—that is, submission and humiliation."[25] But such adoration does not transcend the mediation and the material, for "our worship is an *image* of the eternal reward;"[26] and even in "God too, there are representations and images [*eikones kai paradeigmata*]

---

22. Damascene, *Images III,* 18.
23. Ibid., 3.20.
24. *Latreia* has social and political connotations of "service to one deemed more worthy than oneself." It denotes an active not a passive state.
25. *Images III,* 27.
26. *Images I,* 23. Here, too, the translation appears to have reversed the order found in the Greek.

of His future acts—that is, to say His counsel from all eternity."[27] It may seem that the artist's role is displaced by Christ's work, or even that the artist is redundant, since the task is taken out of his hands because of his inability to execute it. But that reading treats the artist as a distinctive person rather than a mode of seeing and cooperating in the process of holy re-cognition. Abgar desires, he has the vision for what it is he most longs for—to be with Christ. The artist's mode of seeing is different, more profound. The artist sees the form of God' s glory in a mode that can make it more manifest by his or her own making. For it is the artist who re-cognizes that "matter is God's creation and a good thing [*kalen tauten*]"[28] and who, in working with the material honors it. Damascene writes: "I reverence and honor matter, and worship that which has brought about my salvation";[29] "I do not adore creation more than the Creator, but I adore the creature created as I am."[30] A theological aesthetics, inseparable from a theological phenomenology that re-cognizes that all created matter is filled with divine power and grace (*theis energeia kai charis*),[31] begins here. But one has to observe immediately that this aesthetics is not dependent upon the skill of the artist, but on the artist as beholder. What the story illustrates is not the bypassing of the artist as venerator and visionary, but the artist as simply a skillful reproducer, a mechanical reproducer of what is out there. The radiance of Christ's glory reveals that there is nothing outside of Christ; all things are present in Him and are not seized upon by artistic reproduction, but only received as gifts. Therefore, this theological aesthetics that sketches the economy of re-cognition of the

27. *Images II,* 10.
28. *Images II,* 13. The word translated "good" here (*kalon*) can also mean "beautiful," or "pretty" and is homophonic with the more usual word for beautiful *kallon*. See footnote 14 where Plato uses *kalon* for "beauty" in *The Symposium*. Damascene does not use *agathon* and perhaps this suggests the moral order of beauty or the aesthetic order of the good to which he subscribes.
29. *Images II,* 14.
30. *Images I,* 4.
31. *Images I,* 16.

beauty of God, this theological phenomenology, has its foundations in moral theology.[32]

For unlike the post-Kantian phenomenology, a theological phenomenology privileges neither the intentional gaze of the subject (Husserl) nor the primary donation of the object (Marion). Husserl understood the radical immanentalism of phenomenology investigated in this way. Marion, pushes toward an originary donation, a giftedness that bears the trace of a radical transcendence—the radical distance of the Father. But his theological account of phenomenology is still proceeding with Husserlian (and Cartesian) assumptions. The theological phenomenology I am sketching would refuse these assumptions. That we may call this cooperation, or to employ a patristic term *oikonomia,* a phenomenology at all is because it concerns the intentional gaze with respect to making sense of the material order of things. But that gaze and that material order are inseparable when viewed in terms of an incarnational theology and Chalcedon Christology. As one scholar has perceived, with respect to the work of John Damascene: "We find the relationship between the seen and the unseen has been transformed by the incarnation of Christ."[33]

We can take this further, with respect to the object seen, by examining the thought of Theodore of Studion in his *Third Antirrhetici tres adversus iconomachus,* and in particular what has been seen as his major contribution to the theology of icons: understanding the relation between protype and image as a hypostatic one.[34] For Theodore, developing a line of thought in Damascene, hypostasis is the very

---

32. This is not to say the skill of the artist was irrelevant. There is a famous story of Gregory of Nyssa's emotional response to painting of the sacrifice of Isaac (in *On the Divinity of the Son and the Holy Spirit*). Skill was appreciated, but it was secondary so that one might not honor the artist but worship what the icon presents. Damascene quotes Gregory himself writing in the fifth book of his *Structure of Man*: "The divine beauty [*theion kallos*] is not set forth either in form or comeliness of design or colouring, but is contemplated in speechless blessedness, according to its virtue" (*Images I,* 50).

33. Parry, *Depicting the Word,* 37.

34. See G. Ladner, "Origin and Significance of the Byzantine Iconoclastic Controversy," *Mediaeval Studies* 2 (1940): 144.

principle of individuation—that which distinguishes individual substance from species. All things only have individuality insofar as they subsist in Christ. What is phenomenologically received, then, in gazing upon the object is that hypostatic relation that both individuates the things itself and re-cognizes its Christic relation (*schesis*).There is not then a union of natures but a participatory relation (*schetike metalepsis*).[35] Who then is able to see this relation that transforms not the nature (*ousia*) of the object seen but its substance? It is the gaze that is schooled and disciplined in an anagogy, enabling there to be a discernment of "the glorification of matter."[36] But the subject is within the intentional gaze, constituted by it, and likewise the object. The iconic does not therefore announce another phenomenology or an ontological difference that strikes through or "outwits Being,"[37] the finite and all that is idolatrous. We do not "accede, from the very point of view of our situation defined by finitude, to the crossing of Being."[38] For this phenomenological analysis of the icon is founded upon and produces fissures, ruptures and violences within creation. It works in and through dualisms, struggling to attain a point beyond them, a point beyond the phenomenality of the world. It has no understanding of analogy and its necessary relationship to anagogy. Damascene emphasizes that there remains a transcendent distance between the Uncreated God and creation, but it is God Himself who negotiates that distance so that all creation participates within grace and divine power. God descends. As Theodore Abu Qurrah states it: "God made representations with no obvious connection, by means of which what one would do with them would make the contact with that of which they were the representations and images."[39] In one of his letters, Theodore of Studion, developing Aristotelian terminology to define the relation between similarity and difference, speaks in

---

35. *First Antirrheticus* 1.12, *Patrologia Graeca,* XCIX (ed. J-P Migne; Paris, 1857–60); St Theodore of Studion, *On the Holy Icons* (trans. C. P. Roth; New York: St. Vladimir's Seminary Press, 1981).

36. *Images I,* 16.

37. Marion, *God Without Being,* 91.

38. Ibid., 110.

39. Ibid., 62.

terms of an homonymous relation in which Christ and His portrait differ according to their natures (*logos tes ousias*).[40] There is no obvious connection seen from a human perspective. There is no natural affinity between God's self-manifestation and creaturely reality. This is not Stoicism—a difference remains. And yet "what one would do with them" makes possible a re-cognition (what Abu Qurrah calls "contact"). God's condescending grace "stirs us by lifting us up:"[41] kenosis cooperates with anagogy. This is the nature of participation. There are no ruptures, no conflicting ontologies or phenomenologies, no dualisms, only re-cognitions. Dualism is specifically associated with heresies of either a docetic or a Nestorian kind.[42] The idol has no existence, for all things, in God, exist iconically. The artist voices, images, this resurrection song within himself, herself, and all created things. Quoting St. Basil, Damascene writes: "That setting them before us in representation [*dia tes upomneseos koinen*], we are making them helpful to the living, exhibiting their holiness."[43]

The artistic operation, then, remains fundamental to the whole economy of deification. Accounts of the icon made by God circulated from the fifth century, and a tradition grew up of one Ananias who was sent by Abgar and received from Christ a linen cloth he had just used to wipe his face. The Holy Face was imprinted on the cloth in a manner similar to the impression recorded in the fifteenth-century accounts of Veronica's linen towel. But Damascene insists upon the presence and function of the artist,[44] and this is developed theologically by Theodore Abu Qurrah. Damascene himself establishes not only the figure of the artistic mediator but the idea that Abgar desires

---

40.   Letter 528, in *Theodori Studitae Epistulae,* vol. 2 (ed. G. Fatouros; Berlin: Walter de Gruyter, 1991), 790.

41.   Pseudo-Dionysius, *The Celestial Hierarchy,* 1.1; *Pseudo-Dionysius, the Complete Works* (trans. Colm Liubheid; New York: Paulist Press, 1987).

42.   *Images I,* 4.

43.   *Images I,* 44.

44.   1n *Images I,* 33 Damascene gives another rendition of the story, attributing it, perhaps, to Pseudo-Dionysius in *Ecclesiastical Hierarchy.* In this account the "King" of Edessa "sent envoys to ask for his likeness. If this were refused, they were ordered to have a likeness painted." Christ took a strip of

a portrait from Christ.[45] There were, after all, several pagan accounts of statues of the gods that had fallen from the heavens directly. Certain accounts of the power of idols emphasized the lack of human mediation.[46] By changing the traditional account Damascene emphasizes that the revelation of the Christ's transcendent beauty does not bypass human mediation. "I see before me a beautiful picture and the sight refreshes me, and induces me to glorify God."[47]

---

cloth, and pressing it to his face, left His likeness upon it. In this account the artist does not figure and is not required. This is immediately followed by a quotation from a sermon by St. Basil on the martyr St. Barlam, in which Basil calls on "renowned painters" to "set forth by your art a faint image."

45. It is no doubt significant that Damascene was himself a poet/ hymn-writer, the author of a lost "Euripdic" play, *Susana,* and possibly the author of a famous Medieval novel, *Barlaam and Joasaph.* See Moshe Barasch, *Icon: Studies in the History of an Idea* (New York: New York University Press, 1992), 191–92.

46. See Barasch, *Icon,* 40. Of course, in the satire upon idol worship, not only in Biblical satires like Isaiah 44 or Psalm 115, but in classical satires by Heraclitus, Lucian, and Horace, it is the very corruptible materiality and human fashioning of the idol that undermines its divine origin. The Christian account of the icon refuses either extreme, establishing itself on a theological principle of mediation, of a relationship between *methexis* and *mimesis* that baptizes certain Platonic ideas.

47. This use of the word "beautiful" is important. After the great iconoclast controversy, defenders of icons were hesitant about using what today we would call an aesthetic term. Augustine, Pseudo-Dionysius, and Gregory of Nyssa, in their explicit use of "beauty" and the "beautiful" show none of this hesitancy. Damascene will quote Gregory of Nyssa in *Images I,* 41, 42: "The divine beauty is not set forth either in form or comeliness of design or coloring, but is contemplated in speechless blessedness, according to its virtue. So do painters transfer human forms to canvas through certain colors, laying on suitable and harmonious tints to the picture, so as to transfer the beauty of the original to the likeness." It is evident he approves of Gregory's description of the operation of beauty, but it is also evident that there is a lack of confidence about using "beauty" or the "beautiful," perhaps a fear of being misunderstood. After all, Damascene's exile to the monastery of St. Sabbas was possibly related to his condemnation in the Synod 754 by leading iconoclasts for his defense of icons.

The bypassing of mediation pertains to a gnostic logic.[48] The cloth itself is a human artifice. There is hidden in this story the lives of others—not only the citizens whom Abgar represents, but the weavers, the bleachers or dyers, the cotton planters and pickers and spinners. Christ baptizes their endeavors with his own. If you like, they are all artists, for they all make possible the manifestation of Christ's Beauty. The aesthetic stage mediates between Christ the Pantocrator and Abgar the ruler. Christ's operation arises because of what the artist discerns and how he responds to that discernment: "When the artist was unable to do this because of the radiance of His face, the Lord Himself pressed." The artist was only unable to act because he saw "the radiance." His is a privileged position not because of his abilities but because of his proximity and ability to "see the form" (to put it in Balthasarian terms). He beholds the glory of Christ Himself, not the glory of Christ in the cloth. Of course, being an artist he could have painted a portrait, but the stamp of his own integrity, the truth of his own calling, the depth of his own *latreia,* lies in the re-cognition of his inability to paint the glory he sees. The artist lingers on the border between re-cognition and absorption, beholding the deity and being deified.[49] The artist bears witness to

---

48. At the famous Seventh Ecumenical Council of 787 C.E., which reaffirmed following several years of iconoclasm the theological significance of icons, haters of icons were branded with various forms of heresy, among which the gnostic heresies of Manichaeism and Docetism. See Ambrosios Giakalis, *Images of the Divine: The Theology of Icons at the Seventh Ecumenical Council* (Leiden: Brill, 1994), 49. Damascene himself saw iconoclasm as Docetism. See G. Florovsky, *Byzantine Fathers of the Sixth to Eighth Century* (Vaduz: Notable and Academic Books, 1987), 280.

49. A line of thinking opens up here with early discussions of the artist's being "inspired." One thinks of the pneumatologies of Hamann's thinking and Coleridge's. More recently, Austin Farrer in his Bampton Lectures (published as *The Glass of Vision* [Westminster: Dacre Press, 1948]) spoke of how the "choice, use and combination of images made by Christ and the Spirit must be simply a supernatural work. The images were supernaturally formed, and supernaturally made intelligible to faith" (109–10).

the most profound aesthetic operation, what Theodore of Studion termed "the sublime condescension" (*hupsistos sugkatabasis*).[50] It is not simply that the subject of the sentence changes from the artist to Christ. The syntax reflects a more profound ambivalence. When the cloth is sent to Abgar, the text reads "[He, that is Christ] left His own image on the cloth and so sent this." Christ completes the artist's task, but the absence of a personal pronoun with respect to the verb "sent" (the Greek verb is in the infinitive) leaves open which subject performed the action of the sending, Christ or the artist. Abgar receives that for which he asked, but by whose hands does he receive it? Surely it is the artist who delivers, and to all intent and purposes what is he, Abgar, to think but that the artist has fulfilled the task requested of him? The artist fulfils the task by letting Christ take over.[51] Not as one demonically inspired, this is no Platonic or Dionysian fury. The artist relinquishes his skills and labor; he beholds and it is done in all the calm transparency of contemplative prayer. The artist/priest intercedes on behalf of the client that grace may abound. The aesthetic mediates, and this mediation is sanctified because Christ is the fashioner of all things. The artistic operation deepens the appreciation of being made in the image of God; it participates in the ongoing work of incarnation, just as Christ's begottenness is a procession of the Father. The artistic operation deepens the appreciation of the mystery of being human. Neither displaced nor redundant, it fulfils that which is most truly human by participating

50.   *First Antirrhetici,* 1.14. With this use of the sublime, we can put into its historical and cultural context Kantian and post-Kantian notions of sublimity that are examined only in terms of transcendence; ultimately, the transcendence of materiality as such. Here sublimity neither transcends the material, nor saturates it (Jean-Luc Marion's understanding of saturation). The sublime is the condescending assumption and transfiguration of the material by the divine, witnessed by anagogical participation—that is, received by what Damascene's describes as "according to the proportion of faith [*metochoi charitos kata' analogian tes pisteos*]," *Images* 1.36.

51.   See Giakalis, *Images of the Divine,* 62: "a song of the 'assurance' already given by divine grace to the soul of the believers is the very making of the icon."

in a transfigurative work that is ultimately Christic. In his *Homily on the Transfiguration* Damascene argues that the transfiguration of Christ is about the transfiguration of the beholder, such that Christ "renews our nature in himself restoring it to the pristine beauty of the image charged with the common visage of humanity."[52] The artist fulfils the call of being human by receiving this representation and transfiguration of the cloth in his beholding. By that "in" I imply a locational reference, for Damascene would concur with what de Lubac much later informs us about classic Pauline teaching: "Christ appears as a milieu, an atmosphere, a world where man and God, man and man, communicate and are united. He is 'the One who fills and fulfils [*remplit*] all things.'"[53] The artist apprehends in Christ his own humanity, the beauty and perfection of that humanity. It is in that sense that we might say Christ in him fulfils the commission; the artistic operation makes manifest the radiance of Christ. Like the cloth, that which is created comes into its own.

We have Abgar, the artist, and Christ within the story, and I have alluded to the others who wait in the wings (the citizens of Abgar's city, the weavers of the artist's cloth, etc.), but that which makes the story possible at all is the author and the reader. These, too, constitute the manifestation of Christ's beauty. We will treat each separately and unfold something of their distinctive roles in the operation we are discussing. And let us think of the text like that—as an operation, not an object with a message. The author stands in an analogous relationship to the artist as the reader stands in analogous relationship to Abgar. We will treat the author first, though what is of interest to me is the various forms of analogy functioning here, the forms of transferential relation implied in the analogous association. We will return to that.

For simplicity's sake I am equating the author with the implied narrator, though I am aware there is a difference that can be rhetorically

---

52. The French translation of this homily, the only one I am aware of, can be found in R. de Feraudy, ed., *L 'Icone de ta transfiguration, Spirituatite Orientate* 23 (1978): 143.

53. de Lubac, *Catholicisme* (Paris: Les Editions du Cerf, 1965), 30.

employed. The author has a *comprehensive grasp* of the action. Abgar, as I have said, may only understand that the artist has fulfilled his commission, and we are unsure whether the artist fully comprehends the action of Christ with respect to the cloth. The last explicit act of the artist is the recognition of Christ's glory and his inability to depict the face because of it. He does not see the face itself, and in fact none of the people involved in this story see the face of Christ itself. We are treating throughout the effects of Christ's beauty and the dissemination of those effects. We are treating a divine operation, not divinity itself. The author functions to disseminate the effects of that operation. The story stands in analogical relation to the "sending" of the cloth. The storyteller, like the artist, stands before an unfolding event. The narration is simple. It draws no attention to itself rhetorically or stylistically. The author does not appear in person; the authoring is subordinated to the telling. In a sense this story is a representation of various acts of representation, but we are not quite affirming Plato's view of *mimesis* in Book Ten of *Republic*. For the erasure of the authorial position in order to prioritize the telling gives the perspective a certain angelic omniscience. What is achieved through the telling is a matter of whether, as in the story, Christ completes the artist's commission, and presses his face to the tissue of the text. The author makes himself or herself transparent that effects of Christ's beauty might be sent further, passed on.

This leads us to the reader, the one to whom the text is sent, the one who in performing the story (remember, the text is an operation not an object) may disseminate it further. This is what John Damascene does by citing the narrative in his own theological argument; this is what I am doing in giving you an exposition of it. There is a play on the Greek verb *apostello* that means "to send" while simultaneously invoking a reference to the nature of being an apostle, one who is sent. But prior to the sending out is a reception, and it is in that reception that the effects of Christ's beauty are registered. The act of receiving is not simply cognitive. For Damascene the body and the soul profoundly inform each other, for "the soul is united with the body, the entire soul with the entire body, and not part for a part. And it is not contained by the body, but rather contains it."[54] The body then is ensouled. The soul itself possesses two kinds of faculties: the cognitive and the vital. The faculties are related to each other such that cognitive faculties (mind, thought, opinion, imagination, and sensation) serve the will and the making of choices (which are vital or appetitive faculties). Questions concerning the extent to which this account is rendered otiose by more modern conceptions of the mind and cognition need not bother us here. For the main point is that reading, an act of intelligence or any stirring of passion or any sensation whatsoever, involves a "movement of the soul [*kinemapsuches*]."[55] One reads then with body and soul just as in the Eucharist we partake of Christ's two natures, of his body bodily (*somatos somatichos*), and of his divinity spiritually (*theotetos pneumatikos*).[56]

Of course, this is at the heart of what was to develop into the four-folding reading of Scripture, found prior to Damascene in Origen, Cassian, and, in a different form, Augustine.[57] Damascene bequeathed to the defenders of icons in the ninth century the correlation between reading an icon and the spiritual or typological reading of the Scriptures. What connects "image" to "type" is the ability to see the form of Christ; and to see is to be moved inwardly, to re-cognize what Theodore of Studion called "the force of truth."[58] But that seeing takes place first with respect to the body, and so to receive at even the weakest and most simple levels involves the whole person in a transformation, a movement. For example, the reader, like Abgar, desires to know the end of the story if nothing further. Rational desire, for Damascene, is "inherent in the human soul [*egkeitai . . .*

---

54. *De Fide Orthodoxa*, 198.
55. Ibid, 11.22.46, 248.
56. Ibid., 111.26.58–9. For Damascene, as for many of the Church Fathers, the ascended Christ is a Christ who retains embodiment even in heaven. Hence we, too, attain a resurrected corporeality.
57. See Henri du Lubac's magisterial *Mediaeval Exegesis, Volume One: The Four Senses of Scripture* (trans. Mark Sebanc; Grand Rapids: Eerdmans, 1998).
58. See *Third Antirrhetici*, 1.1, *On Holy Icons*.

tou anthropou psuche dunamis]."[59] The reader, like Abgar, receives a gift, and the question is now whether the reader, like Abgar, has the capacity to receive the gift. The question of the beauty of God is inseparable not only from a thinking through of the gift, of donation, but a thinking through of reception. To receive the gift is to enter that mode of apprehension in which one recognizes the face of Christ. Any other handling of the text, as any other handling of the "bit of cloth," fails to receive because it fails to re-cognize that a gift has been given and the nature of that gift and giving. The questions of how to receive and how to recognize or, to reverse the order (for I would question whether these are two distinct events, chronologically related), the questions of how to recognize and how to receive are questions concerning discipleship.

To explore this further we need to step back from our exegesis of the story and ask about what is recognized and what is received; to enquire into a pedagogy of desire such that we can re-cognize and re-ceive. For to re-cognize and to re-ceive imply, in the way I have inflected them, a recovery of that which was already possessed. The nature of discipleship is such that one is enabled to recover a lost perspective. In brief, the beauty we apprehend is ultimately the re-cognition of ourselves and all creation in Christ. For we cannot receive the beauty of God itself, being human. We can only receive the beauty of God in relation to the world He has created. We are not transported beyond this world into some pure and immediate relation to divinity. We are returned to the world more profoundly by the beautiful. We re-cognize and re-ceive the paradisial, the perfected. Discipleship, as the training and disciplining of desire such that our actions are ever-increasingly dictated by our desire for God, trains us for redemption—re-demption, re-cognition, re-ception. Discipleship returns us to where we are in God; where all creation is in God. Maybe this is why the artist stands before the beauty of God and can do nothing. For to portray one has to see and place that act of seeing at a certain distance; one sees the beauty, and then

---

59. *De Fide Orthodoxa*, n. 22.62, 249.

one depicts the beauty. But if to see the beautiful is to see all things perfected in Christ, to see one's own perfection in Christ then, in a sense, one no longer sees the beautiful for one is beautiful. Nothing remains to be done with this beauty but to enjoy it. Ascesis gives way to pleasure. No space is possible for a viewing or depicting. With what would one depict? The cloth itself, the paints, the quarried rock, the musical notes would all be in themselves perfectly beautiful—they would be placed beyond being used as tools by their very perfection. Furthermore, enjoying their perfection would be inseparable from enjoying one's own perfection in relation to these things. We are getting closer here to what is it that is re-cognized, what is it that is re-ceived. And we are returning to those complex levels of analogy I sketched, those relations. For that is what analogies constitute: webs of relation and differences. What is re-cognized, then, in the apprehension of the beauty of God, is the constitution of beauty itself. That is, how all things are not only perfected in Christ, but in the particularity of their giftedness they are interdependent and compose the body of Christ. Put in another way, one re-cognizes the perfection of all distinct things in re-cognizing their co-constitution. Beauty is manifest as both perfecting the particular, rendering it beautifully distinct and as a order, sustained and commanded by Christ. Analogical relations portray both difference and ordering. In this way cosmology is closely connected to aesthetics.[60]

But to apprehend the relations requires more than just being told they are there. Analogy is not a teaching, nor a manner of teaching to be learned and applied by human beings. What is analogically related is made manifest. We *receive* analogy. We are able to receive in this way because, first, we are ourselves analogical in being *made in the*

---

60. I am agreeing here with Alejandro Gracia-Rivera, in his book, *The Community of the Beautiful: A Theological Aesthetics* (Collegeville, Minn.: The Liturgical Press, 1999), 70. I share many of Garcia-Rivera' s emphases and convictions, but where he begins his investigations with Balthasar's work, I prefer to examine the texts in the tradition that Balthasar gave little attention to for all his concern to develop a theological aesthetics.

image of[61] and, secondly, the process of discipleship is anagogical. The analogical relations and the anagogical process are themselves nothing other than the operations of the divine within creation. The analogical world-view is not a system, and the anagogical process cannot be regulated, not for John Damascene, and not for the Cappadocian fathers. Analogical systems and guides to personal progress, the whole *scientia spiritualis,* come later.[62] The ordered operations of the divine are made manifest in the re-cognition and re-ception of the beautiful but we cannot grasp these operations as such; they are beyond codification. We cannot determine and thereby manipulate them in any way. We can only receive them. The relation between Abgar as lord of the city and Christ as Lord of creation, and the relation of Abgar's sending to Christ's sending are both established through the repetition of the word. The relations are not explained. What the story demonstrates is the power of one with respect to the desire and needs of the other. And yet, Damascene emphasizes that we are to reason about these things. The story is an intelligible form appealing to intelligibility. The work of the artist cannot complete the task commanded but that does not mean the work is irrelevant, as I have argued above. The artist's task is completed *through* his contemplation of the radiance of Christ's face *in* his participation in the radiance of Christ's own glory, *by* being made beautiful in Christ's Beauty. We are to seek understanding not for its own sake but in order to enter more fully into what is given in the divine operation itself. As such, the manifestation of the beautiful is not an end in itself, an object to be owned in Abgar's case; it is a means of developing a mode of living in relation to the mode of apprehension. The

---

61. Etymologically, the word *anthropos* is derived from *ano throsko*—"I look upwards." Theodore of Studion makes this teaching explicit in his *Third Antirrheticus* in which the work of image-making itself is a divine activity (*deiknusi theion ti chrema uparchein to tes eikonourgias eidos*), (III.2.A5).

62. See Michael de Certeau, *The Mystic Fable: The Sixteenth and Seventeenth Centuries* (trans. Michael B. Smith; Chicago: University of Chicago Press, 1992), 79–112.

operation is salvific; participation in a movement of return to the enjoyment of "everlasting bliss";[63] part of a transformation, a *metanoia*. In the tenth century, we find Andrew of Crisi explaining that the beauty (*kallos*) of the icon is not in the form (*schema*) nor in the bright colors, but in the "ineffable beatitude of represented virtue" (*all 'en aphrasto makarioteti kata areten theoreitai*).[64] Discerning the beautiful as the analogical ordering of the world with respect to the Word is a profoundly moral activity. It does not foster out-of-the-body experiences, nor a renunciation of the corporeal. The ensoulment of the body means that the more profound the participation in the divine, the more intensely the body becomes what it is. The disciplining of the body is to give it greater attention, to focus precisely its delights and limitations. As Damascene observes of Adam: "This man He set in paradise which was both of the mind and of the sense. Thus, while in his body he lived on earth in the world of the sense, in his spirit he dwelt among the angels, cultivating thoughts of God and being nurtured on these."[65] Contemplation, the employment of reason, in a rational desire to seek the good and the beautiful in Christ, is a "nurturing"—an activity.

The manifestation of beauty and its apprehension are part of an ongoing transforming activity. The analogical order of relations is apprehended by and fosters anagogical practice. At the heart of this practice is a *making*, a fashioning, a *poeisis*: The artist, the author, the reader, the patron, and commissioner have their part to play in this creativity, this cultivation of the thoughts of God. Anagogy is the development of a lifestyle, an aesthetics of living in which to apprehend the beautiful is to become beautiful. One practices beauty in a movement of redemption from purification and illumination to glorification and doxology. This is what John Damascene was doing, living in the desert outside Jerusalem, in that monastery still to be seen today, the monastery of St. Sabbas perched above a narrow canyon of sun white rock. The operation of beauty is to beautify; its intellectual

---

63. *De Fide Orthodoxa*, II.30.33, 265.
64. Quoted in Parry, *Depicting the Word*, 92–93.
65. *De Fide Orthodoxa*, II.30.21–7, 265.

content is the re-cognition of relations in their gifted particularity. Neither operation nor cognition of the beautiful is an end in itself. The operation and apprehension is an education concomitant with discipleship involving two distinct stages: (a) remembrance of what one has been taught of the faith; (b) and the disciplining of desire so that it becomes rational.[66] To become beautiful is to be schooled into choosing well. Theological aesthetics cannot be divorced from ethics; what is appreciated cannot be separated from who is appreciating it, by what means, with what effects. As I stated earlier, with respect to introducing and justifying my exegesis, the manifestation of the beauty of God has a constitution, and so does the apprehension of that manifestation. Both are part of beauty as an operation.

Several corollaries follow from this account of the beautiful, and I will point at three. First, art is not intrinsically theological. At least not in any direct sense. A work of art may possess certain properties, of form, or color, or texture, that trigger psychosomatic experiences of wonder, harmony or dis-ease. A work of art may trigger experiences that, since the late eighteenth and nineteenth centuries, we have come to associate with the religious, the spiritual—experiences that transport us or expand our consciousness of the world and ourselves. But the account of the beautiful I am giving here would distinguish between the warm (or foreboding) feelings that are described as religious or spiritual and the theological apprehension of the beauty of God. That a work of human creation participates in the operation of the divine

---

66. The deliberations of the Seventh Ecumenical Council provide an account of these two distinct operations: "Such a beholding urges him who has received the deeds of holy men through hearing about them to remembrance of what he has heard, and prepares him who is ignorant to them to inquire after them and being instructed in them stirs him warmly to the desire for them and praise of God, so that through both of these, those who behold the good works of the saints should praise our Father in heaven." (Giakalis, *Images of the Divine,* 57). The language of anagogy is the language of ascent through sensible images to divine contemplation. See Pseudo-Dionysius *On the Eccl. Hier.* 1.2. Memory of the prototypes incites the desire for them. Theology is constituted as *memoria.*

and that there is a discernment of that operation does not imply that the divine is intrinsic to the work. There is no direct connection, only a mediated one. But the nature of this mediation is such that the work is not simply a vehicle for the operation. The mediation is at the heart of the incarnation: God becoming human. The mediation is also at the heart of the human capacity to recognize the incarnational: that is, that we are made *in the image* of God. More space would be needed to explicate this important difference between religious aesthetics and theological aesthetics. But, primarily, beauty as a co-operative operation (a *synergia*) rather than a property (a theological account of aesthetics) implies that there is nothing that cannot be made to tender its beauty as the beauty of God. All is in the mode of apprehension, participation, and the anagogical practice that has taught the recipient how to receive (that is, discern). The face of Christ can be found in what, to the unschooled, would be brutal and ugly. We might recall what Balthasar said about the faces of Christ in the clowns of Georges Rouault: "It takes the eye of faith to see in Christ the humiliation and offending of eternal love and in one's disfigured fellow human beings the glimmer of grace."[67] A Christian aesthetics is founded upon the implications of the incarnation.[68]

But we can take this much further, as Balthasar would do. This would be my second corollary. The operation of the beautiful overrides purely aesthetic emphases upon the present pleasure of what is seen or heard or tasted. In fact, the orthodox theology of icons downplayed such aesthetic values. The present sensual experience was not something consumed in and of itself. The apprehension of beauty transcended sensual tastes or subjective judgments, transcended connoisseurship or aesthetic expertise. The consumption of immediate, one might almost say naïve, appreciations of color, line, harmonies, counterpoint, and balances would be an act of profound

---

67. *The Realm of Metaphysics in the Modern Age* (vol. 5 of *The Glory of the Lord: A Theological Aesthetics;* ed. Hans Urs Von Balthasar et al.; trans. Oliver Davies et al.; Edinburgh: T&T Clark, 1991), 203.

68. See Jaroslav Pelikan, *Imago Dei: The Byzantine Apologia for Icons* (Princeton: Princeton University Press, 1990), 67–98.

disrespect for what was truly beautiful. What is consumed are simply the properties of an object. Such an act abuses the object by turning it into an idol and making it occasion for evil. The object is reified and fetishized.

The Seventh Ecumenical Council of 787 C.E., which made its ruling on icons, affirmed that the "representation of things which have no being is called idolatrous."[69] Similarly the appreciation of an object for its sensual dimensions alone brings "non-existent things into existence." It is making the object something that it is not; it deprives it of its true being. As such, that privation of being, which is a privation also of good, is an evil act. Beauty does not lie merely in its sensual dimensions. Conversely, as John Damascene writes, "the art of him who draws always contribut[es] to the service of reality." This is a fundamental insight. The sensual dimensions are not erased or viewed as insignificant, either in the aesthetic operation or the one who receives the effects of that operation. Their significance is greatly heightened, as I pointed out, by apprehending those dimensions in the light of that which gives them their distinctive significance and order. In fact, artistic work not only renders the truly beautiful real, but it renders the real itself. Christian *poeisis* creates the reality of all things. It participates in the ongoing divine activity of redeeming the world by creating an "orthodox realism."[70] *Theoria* and *poeisis,* the pillars of a theological phenomenology, are profoundly implicated in *theosis.* To use an important word in English Renaissance aesthetics, one can delight in the truly sensuous only when one's understanding is illuminated by the radiance of heavenly beauty. What becomes evident thereby is the inseparability of a Christian aesthetics from a Christian epistemology, and both from a theological ethics.

Much can, I suggest, be understood about the changes wrought by modernity (and by implication, postmodernity) by observing the way "illumination" becomes "enlightenment" and "enlightenment" becomes "'erring." In some sense we can see the Kantian triptych— the critiques of pure reason, practical reason, and judgment—as a

69. Quoted in Giakalis, *Images of the Divine,* 89.
70. Ibid., 89.

nod toward the inseparability of epistemology, ethics, and aesthetics. But their increasing separation and autonomy as fields of enquiry were already well under way for there was nothing now to hold them together. Participation and what John Chrysostom had termed *logike latreia*[71] had been replaced by epistemology as a foundational science, knowledge was divorced from being, and the subject over against the object had been installed. The postmodern aestheticization of all knowledge, which recognizes knowledge as political but not ethical, and the postmodern pragmatics, which encourages the aesthetic cultivation of temporary "lifestyles" without virtue, demonstrate the inevitable shift from "enlightenment" to "erring." While the sixteenth-century English poet Edmund Spenser is only continuing this Patristic tradition of appreciating the beauty of God, only continuing the artist's mediation that gives way to an act of heavenly grace, when he writes in his poem "An Hymne in Honour of Beautie":

> Queene of Beauty,
> Mother of love, and of all worlds delight,
> Without whose soverayne grace and kindly dewty
> Nothing on earth seems fayre to fleshly sight,
> Doe thou vouchsafe with thy love-kindling light
> T' illuminate my dim and dulled eynes,
> And beautifie this sacred hymne of thyne.

In Christ, the production of the visible from its physiology, to its psychology and its symbolization, is sanctified.[72]

---

71. *Homilies of the Romans* XX.2 (vol. 11 of *The Nicene and Post-Nicene Fathers of the Christian Church*; Grand Rapids: Eerdmans, 1979), 497.

72. For the historical development of this theological understanding of sense-perception (*aesthesis*), see Pelikan, *Imago Dei,* 99–120; James Trilling's very suggestive account in "The Image Not Made by Hands and the Byzantine Way of Seeing" in Kessler and Wolf, *The Holy Face and the Paradox of Representation,* 109–27; and Herbert L. Kessler, *Spiritual Seeing: Picturing God's Invisibility in Medieval Art* (Philadelphia: University of Pennsylvania Press, 2000), 104–48.

Finally, thirdly, what this account of the beauty of God provides is an insight into the very mystery of the Godhead. For the economy of participation has the structure of a certain irony. This is not a romantic dialectical irony, but the irony that pertains to that which in being most itself calls forth also its mystery as being wholly other. It is the irony evident in Paul's statement "Christ in me the hope of glory," where what is most truly human is also a manifestation of glory of Christ. It is the irony of being both oneself and another in Christ, the irony of being created "in the image of." But what does this irony deliver, theologically, if not the irony at the heart of triunity where difference not only remains unsublated but is actually constituted as difference in relation. The Spirit continually draws us forth in acts interpreting the mystery of that which, in being itself, is also an intimation of the mystery of otherness. That at the heart of the beauty of God lies a profound irony, that irony might be understood as an intimation of divinity, leaves each of us suspended in so much that is understood (re-cognized) while not being grasped. Suspended in the experience of seeing through a glass darkly, laboring in an ineradicable hope, and glimpsing in the beauty of God that there is nothing, then, that cannot be redeemed.[73]

---

73. And, therefore, I would say Marion was wrong to insist that the idol is "*se ferme a tout autre*" (*La Croisée du visible*, 121). For no object is shut up within itself in such a way that the participating, co-operating gaze cannot open it up, enabling it to blossom. To reiterate what I said, rehearsing the judgment of the Seventh Ecumenical Council, the idol is nothing, it is a fantasy. There is no idol.

3

Between Swooners and Cynics
The Art of Envisioning God

Edith Wyschogrod

The semiotic possibilities of the Hebrew of Gen 1:31, *Viyar Elohim et kol asher asa vehinei tov meod* ("God saw everything that he had made and indeed it was very good"), include cognitive, moral, and aesthetic dimensions. Some traditional interpretations see the text as asserting that the world is well-wrought, that nature's means, cunningly adapted to its ends, are indications of divine purposiveness and that obedience to divine ordinances is a manifestation of human goodness. Other accounts focus upon the created order as a vast spectacle that attests nature's power to arouse awe and rapture, a perspective reflected in the Romantic coupling of art and nature. Thus F. W. J. Schelling, in a lecture of 1804, declares: "The universe is formed in God as an absolute work of art and in eternal beauty . . . beauty in which infinite intention interpenetrates infinite necessity."[1]

Does the Romantic rapture of this Schellingian pronouncement not wend its way into postmodernity in the gaze of the tourist who

---

1. F. W. J. Schelling, *The Philosophy of Art* (Theory and History of Literature, vol. 58; trans. Douglas W. Stott; Minneapolis: University of Minnesota Press, 1989), 31.

inwardly cordons off the admiring hordes to proclaim the beauty of that primordial beginning as rendered by Michelangelo or Giovanni di Paolo? Is there a connection between God envisaged as creator and the ascription of beauty? Is the link understood as one of direct agency? These questions presuppose a way of seeing hidden in our manner of questioning, in our comportments toward what is viewed as beautiful. Thus the wide-eyed ecstatic whom I shall hereafter refer to as the "swooner" asks, "*Ah* what is beauty *really,*" while the doubting protester whom, in conformity with an ancient philosophical tradition, I shall call the "cynic," inquires disparagingly, "What is beauty *anyway?*"

I shall not try to determine why some things rather than others may be called beautiful or to weigh received accounts of beauty. Instead, I shall focus on the world orientations or dispositions of the questioner, the "ah" of the swooner and the "anyway" of the cynic, as each encounters the referent of the term *beauty.* By tracking the philosophical matrices from which these perspectives derive, I hope to show that swooners and cynics cannot do without one another if the extremes of näiveté and nihilism are to be avoided and that each must be taken into account in speaking about God. I shall consider how the disruption of the cynic erupts into the beautiful, disfigures it, but in so doing helps to transfigure it and shall conclude by describing some ways in which theological thinking is bound up with both.

SWOONING AND THE SUBLIME

It might be thought that swooning before the artwork or the phenomena of nature can be traced to *thaumazein,* the Greek term for wonder or amazement referred to in the philosophies of Plato and Aristotle. But the view that swooning is allied to wonder is, in part, the result of an often unacknowledged redescription of the Greek *thaumazein* by a nineteenth-century Romantic aesthetic. Considered as a devaluing of the world and a plunging into an inner world, the Romantic aesthetic, as depicted by its adversaries, is the very opposite of the serenity of the ancients. Thus, Schelling discerns in the aesthetics of his contemporaries characteristics the ancients had censured, "audacious fire, and violent, shrieking, fleeting antitheses." Or, as Johann Joachim Winckelmann declares: "One finds oneself as if at a party where everyone wants to talk at once."[2]

It goes without saying that accounts of beauty abound in Plato, Aristotle, and their immediate successors but, as Schelling had already noticed, the claim that for classical thought the beholder dissolves into ecstasy before that which is beautiful must be dismantled. Accordingly, the notion that swooning began in Athens requires revision. To be sure, Plato describes an eager young man, Theatetus, in the dialogue of that name as "astonished." It is not however beauty but "the ridiculous and wonderful contradictions" of ordinary speech that became grist for the mill of the sophists that are the sources of his astonishment. "I am amazed . . . my head quite swims with the contemplation of [their questions]," Theatetus exclaims. For Socrates, the young man's amazement proves that he is a true philosopher and leads Socrates to announce: "For wonder [*thaumazein*] is the feeling of a philosopher, and philosophy begins in wonder."[3] Lest we identify wonder with affect, with what the swooner feels, recall that the *thaumazein* of Theatetus is bound up with intellect, with attempting to settle the logical disputes of the sophists.

Socrates is not, however, insensitive to the ambiguities inherent in his own account, conceding that beauty crosses the line from the world of the senses and physical pleasures to that of mind. Consider Socrates' quandary in *Philebus* 66: "Has mind a greater share of beauty than pleasure, and is mind or pleasure the fairer [more beautiful] of the two?" His respondent, Protarchus, admits that certain pleasures make us ashamed, so "we put them out of sight, consign them to darkness" and turn instead to "the eternal nature of measure and the mean." Socrates is forced to acknowledge that "there are pleasures that accompany the sciences and those that accompany the senses,

2.   Ibid., 154. Winckelmann is cited by Schelling.
3.   Plato, *Theatetus,* 155 (vol. 2 of *The Dialogues of Plato*; trans. Benjamin Jowett; New York: Random House, 1937), 157.

and that both pleasure and mind are wanting in self-sufficiency."[4] Is there, in the admission that mind is not self-sufficient, a certain return of the repressed, a pleasure of the senses that cannot be eliminated? Unsurprisingly, Socrates concludes that mind is far ahead.

Continuing Plato's line of thought, Aristotle, in what is by now a truism, declares:

> It is owing to their wonder that men both now begin and at first began to philosophize. They wondered originally at the obvious difficulties [and advanced to greater matters] e.g. the phenomena of the moon and those of the sun and of the stars and about the genesis of the universe.[5]

Stunned by the mystery and sheer magnitude of what they saw, even the lovers of myth sought to flee their ignorance. Aristotle insists that he does not mean to reinstate the näiveté of those who wonder about "self-moving marionettes, or the solstices, or the incommensurability of the diagonal of a square with the side."[6] Rather, he contends, in order to escape from ignorance one should seek to know the *causes* of things.

If not in the world of ancient Athens, where then, and when, are the voices of the swooners first heard, the "Ah" that persists in the aesthetic predilections of postmodern times? I shall not enter into the question of the cultural determinants that may have generated the gasp before the Gothic cathedral or the water lilies of Monet, the fjords of Norway or the peaks of the Himalayas. Nor shall I ask how the beauty of a fragment isolated in a moment of emotion, of pristine aesthesis, may be inwardized and saved. Needless to say, the *thaumazein* of the classical world passed through a long and troubled history before wonder became awe in the face of "beauty without limit."

---

4.   Ibid., 402–3.
5.   Aristotle, *Metaphysics,* 982b (*The Basic Works of Aristotle*; trans. Richard McKeon; New York: Random House, 1941), 692.
6.   Ibid.

In response to the veneration of the plastic arts and poetry of the Greeks, one nineteenth-century critic, Paul Friedrich Richter, dismisses the ineluctable nostalgia for what is irretrievable. Realizing that we can no more reexperience the classical past in its own being than we can repeat fleeting natural phenomena, Richter maintains: "Duplication of a whole people would be a greater wonder than a fantastic sky of clouds completely matching some former sky. Not even in Greece could antiquity be resurrected."[7]

The limitless beauty rhapsodized by Richter's contemporaries is seen by him as "the romantic, the undulant hum of a vibrating string or bell whose sound waves fade away into ever greater distances and is finally lost in ourselves."[8] While he acknowledges a Romantic impulse in other times and places, he finds its quintessential expression in Christianity, especially in the Marian piety of southern Europe. Thus Richter states:

> The peerless Mary endows all women with Romantic nobility; a Venus is merely beautiful, but a madonna is Romantic. This higher love is . . . the very blossom or flower of Christianity, which with its ardent zeal in opposing the earthly dissolves the beautiful body into the beautiful soul in order to love the body in the soul, the beautiful in the infinite.[9]

To understand the onset of the great wash of feeling in the presence of the beautiful in modernity, we must look to the philosophy of Immanuel Kant. How, it might be asked, could the sober Kant so opposed to what he called *Schwermerei*, to the *Sturm und Drang* mindset exhibited by some of his contemporaries, have furthered the interest of the swooners? Was he not so practical as to have said,

---

7.   Jean Paul Friedrich Richter, "School for Aesthetics," in *German Romantic Criticism* (ed. Ernst Behler; trans Margaret R. Hale; vol. 21 of The German Library; New York: Crossroads, 1982), 47.

8.   Ibid., 50.

9.   Ibid., 52.

"What a pity that the lilies do not spin?"[10] and so work-obsessed that he changed his lodgings when a neighbor refused to do away with the noisy rooster that disturbed his philosophical speculations?[11] I shall not delve into the details of Kant's life for fear of drifting into ad hominem arguments and shall turn instead to his *Third Critique,* a work whose purpose can be seen as bridging the gulf between theoretical and practical reason, between the knowledge of nature and the moral life.

What Kant calls the understanding provides us with a grid prior to experience through which we acquire a knowledge of nature as an object of sense.[12] By contrast, practical or moral reason is "the supersensible in the subject" (*CJ,* 32). Prior to all experience, practical reason legislates in the moral realm and has pride of place in that it can prescribe limits to the understanding. The gulf between what we tend to call fact and value may seem unbridgeable, but Kant thinks nature has a purpose and that we can find in the understanding of nature a way of bringing the two together. The purposiveness of nature can be grasped in a twofold way, first, as having to exist in conformity with the concept of freedom, and second, as a certain possibility presupposed in nature, namely the nature of the human being as a sensible being (*CJ,* 32). What is important for my argument is Kant's claim that there is a special pleasure in the apprehension of nature as having a purpose even if we cannot know this purpose.

---

10. J. H. W. Stuckenberg, *The Life of Immanuel Kant* (London: Macmillan, 1882).

11. Arseniz Glyga, *Immanuel Kant: His Life and Thought* (trans. Marijan Despalatovic; Boston: Birkhauser, 1985), 84.

12. Immanuel Kant, *Critique of Judgment* (trans. J. H. Bernard; New York: Hafner Press, 1951). Cited in the text as *CJ.* In considering the unity of the system's parts in the *Third Critique,* Gary Banham in *Kant and the Ends of Aesthetics* (New York: St. Martin's Press, 2000) claims Kant resolves the problem of uniting nature and freedom through a procedure of analogy: "Critical analogy is analogy by type of comparison with form. Causality of freedom is not the same kind of causality as natural causality . . . [T]he type of form is all that is involved in the procedure of analogy [and] is what permits unity between the three parts of the critical system" (164).

When judged subjectively prior to any concept, purposiveness is the subject of aesthetic judgments; when judged objectively as the harmony of a thing's concept with its form, it is the subject of what Kant calls teleological judgments (*CJ*, 29). In aesthetic judgments, we judge the object to be purposive but are unable to explain its purpose so that we experience a purposiveness without purpose as in apprehending the beauty of a tree, a bird of paradise, or as he disconcertingly suggests, the beauty of foliage on wallpaper (*CJ*, 66). In the case of teleological judgment, we actually know what the object's purpose is.

This distinction between types of judgment provides the ground for Kant's account of beauty. When the form of an object is merely reflected upon without reference to a concept and is judged as the ground of pleasure, it is called beautiful and the faculty of judging such an object, taste (*CJ*, 28). But the pleasure I experience when seeing the beautiful object is necessarily private. If a judgment of taste is based on private experience, is it possible to secure agreement about judgments of taste? Yet such judgments are valid for all, according to Kant, because there is a subjective yet common ground for them, a sense common to all (*sensus communis*). Still, agreement about what is beautiful secured through a judgment, albeit a judgment of taste, can hardly be expected to give rise to swooning.

Not only must the reception of the artwork be considered, but also the role of the artist. The creator of the artwork that is not merely pleasant but purposive in itself calls for greatness in the artist. Such a work requires "genius . . . the innate mental disposition (*ingenium*) through which nature gives the rule to art" (*CJ*, 150). Because artistic talent is itself a natural faculty, genius must be seen as a natural gift. Although in the realm of morality, Kant appeals to the universality of law, he insists that no rule can be given for creating a work of genius. "Hence originality must be its first property" (*CJ*, 150). Artistic skill cannot be transmitted but dies with the artist. Even if the work of the artist is not one of unfettered imagination but rather of imagination constrained by understanding (*CJ*, 152), Kant nevertheless makes extraordinary claims for the power of imagination:

> [As] the productive faculty of cognition [imagination]
> is very powerful in creating another nature, as it were,
> out of the material that actual nature gives it. We enter-
> tain ourselves with it when experience becomes too
> commonplace and by it we remold experience . . .
> working up [this material] into something that sur-
> passes nature." (*CJ*, 157)

Nietzsche remains Kant's successor when he proclaims, "Artists should see nothing as it is, but fuller, simpler, stronger: to that end, their lives must contain a kind of youth and spring, a kind of habitual intoxication."[13] Thus, despite Nietzsche's critique of what he saw as residual Christian belief in Kant's view of the moral law and his contention that Kant remained untouched by the beauty of antiquity, praise for the imagination of the genius enters in scarcely altered form into his own thought.

But the genius of the artist does not of itself suffice to account for the emergence of the swoon of the viewer. Kant must first explain the difference between the beautiful and what he calls the sublime. Beauty inheres in the form of the object and is discovered through quiet contemplation whereas the sublime, by contrast, is formless, exhibits no purpose, and is apprehended in a state of excitation, "a momentary checking of the vital powers and a consequent stronger outflow of them" (*CJ*, 83). Judgments of sublimity are universally valid, disinterested, necessary, and exhibit subjective purposiveness, claims that are perplexing in that the object of such judgments is formless and the state of the subject is one of excitation. The claim of universality can, however, be accounted for as depending upon the supersensible, upon moral feeling.

Kant goes on to distinguish between the mathematical sublime, that of magnitude, and the dynamical sublime, that of power. With

---

13. Friedrich Nietzsche, *The Will to Power* 801(trans. Walter Kaufmann and R. J. Hollingdale; New York: Vintage Books, 1968), 421. For his criticism of Kant, see 101, p. 64.

regard to the former, we try to think that which is not merely great but absolutely great. Because we perceive that sensible standards cannot measure infinite magnitude, we are left with a feeling of pain but, at the same time, the sheer attempt to think the sublime excites in us the "feeling of a supersensible faculty" (*CJ,* 88). Kant explains:

> The mind feels itself moved in the representation of the sublime in nature, while in aesthetic judgments about the beautiful it is in *restful* contemplation. This movement may . . . be compared to a vibration, an alternating attraction towards and repulsion from the same object. (*CJ,* 97)

When nature is interpreted as might, as power that arouses fear but nevertheless has no dominion over us, it is understood as dynamically sublime (*CJ,* 99). Consider Kant's example:

> Bold, overhanging, and as it were threatening rocks; clouds piled up in the sky, moving with lightning flashes and thunder peals; volcanoes in all their violence of destruction; hurricanes with their track of devastation, the boundless ocean in a state of tumult; the lofty waterfall of a mighty river . . . these exhibit our faculty of resistance as insignificantly small in comparison with their might. But the sight of them is the more attractive, the more fearful it is, provided only that we are in security. (*CJ,* 100)

I can think of no better illustration of Kant's account than the well-known painting *Man Viewing Storm at Sea* by Caspar David Friedrich. A figure is standing on a cliff, his back toward the viewer and from the relative safety of this vantage point, looks out at an infinite expanse of raging sea that seems to retreat into the depths of the painting. It could be argued that Friedrich's work exhibits a form of Romanticism denigrated by Nietzsche when he wrote: "A romantic is an artist whose great dissatisfaction with himself makes him creative—who looks away, looks back from himself and from his world."[14]

There is, however, a more troubling example of the sublime adduced by Kant—its concrete historical embodiment in war. Kant, an admirer of the French Revolution but also a defender of peace, remarks, "War, if it is carried on with order and with a sacred respect for the rights of citizens, has something sublime in it" (*CJ*, 102).[15] Such Kantian niceties as the rights of the citizen vanish in Nietzsche's praise for the sheer exhilaration of war. "In times of painful tension and vulnerability," Nietzsche urges, "choose war: it hardens, it produces muscle,"[16] an outcome whose desirability would hardly have been sanctioned by Kant.

AFTER ECSTASY: CYNICISM AS CRITIQUE

Having traced the route of the swooner to the threshold of postmodernity, I can now turn to the path of the cynic. Is cynicism a necessary moment that disrupts the swoon, thereby casting a pall over ecstasy or can ecstasy reassert itself? It might be thought that the spoilers of swooning would be found not among the cynics but rather among the ancient skeptics such as Carneades (214–129 B.C.E.), who held that there is no way to distinguish fantastic from allegedly true representations and, when forced to respond to those who said this view would paralyze action, proposed a doctrine of probability.[17]

---

14. Nietzsche, *The Will to Power* 844, 445.

15. A comparable view can be found in Immanuel Kant, *On History* (trans. Lewis White Beck; New York: Liberal Arts Press, 1963), 19. For the way in which the Kantian dynamical sublime figures in the conception of the historical subject see Edith Wyschogrod, *The Ethics of Remembering: History, Heterology and the Nameless Others* (Chicago: University of Chicago Press, 1998), 41–68.

16. Nietzsche, *The Will to Power* 1040, 535.

17. See Michael Frede, "The Sceptic's Two Kinds of Assent," in *The Original Sceptics: A Controversy* (ed. Myles Burnyeat and Michael Frede; Indianapolis: Hackett Publishing Company, 1997), 141.

The physician and skeptic Sextus Empiricus (ca. 250 C.E.) argued that skeptics lay out conflicting accounts of opposing appearances or ideas with each account being equally convincing. This strategy leads to a suspension of judgment so that in any opposed pair of accounts, neither alternative is accepted or rejected. Skeptics may assent to the feelings forced upon them by appearances, feelings that are passive and unwilled but will make no claims about the relation of these appearances to external objects. Judgment is also suspended in moral matters, in that those who hold that some things are good and others bad are perpetually distressed and fail to attain the serenity thought to be desirable.[18] What troubled the ancient skeptics, some scholars argue, are not perceived contradictions but rather the claims that are made for the basic assumptions or the framework within which dogmatic philosophers work. Rather than demolishing all claims to knowledge, the skeptics refine them, paring away misleading affirmations by suspending judgment about the trustworthiness of our knowledge beyond that which appears.[19]

To track the genealogy of later critiques of swooning, we must look not to the skeptics but to the ancient cynics, those wild men who are said to have lived vagrant lives, assaulted established values, called attention to themselves through imaginative gestures of protest. They stressed acts rather than discourses, although recent scholarship suggests that their imaginative improvisations generated new literary forms, i.e. burlesques and parodies.[20] Consider first the crafty cynic Diogenes of Sinope (413–323 B.C.E.) as a conceptual persona, a phrase coined by French philosopher Gilles Deleuze to

---

18. Sextus Empiricus, *Outlines of Skepticism,* Bk. I, iv–xiii (trans. Julia Annas and Jonathan Barnes; Cambridge: Cambridge University Press, 1994), 4–12.

19. This is the position of Michael Freyde in "The Sceptic's Two Kinds of Ascent," in Burnyeat and Frede, *The Original Sceptics,* 153.

20. R. Bracht Branham, "Defacing the Currency: Diogenes' Rhetoric and the Invention of Cynicism," in *The Cynics* (ed. R. Bracht Branham and Marie Odile Goulet-Caze; Berkeley: University of California Press, 1996), 83–85.

mean the specific nexus of concepts laid out by a thinker as generally signalled by her or his proper name, rather than the thinker as an existing individual.[21]

According to legend, Diogenes lived in the Greek-speaking town of Sinope on the Turkish coast of the Black Sea where his father, Hicesius, was in charge of issuing the city's currency. Charged with altering the legal tender of Sinope either by counterfeiting or in some way defacing it, Diogenes is forced into exile. His gesture is confirmed by the oracle of Delphi who tells him "Falsify," a command that leads him to reorient his life so that he tests the mores of his society as one tests coins to see whether they are genuine. In defacing the values of his day, Diogenes acquires the title "The Dog" because it is known that dogs recognize friends who, for Diognes, are those suited to philosophy, and enemies those whom dogs drive away.[22] Philosophy is not equated with Plato's account of ideal forms but rather with a concern for the concrete particulars of life. In fact, Diogenes is alleged to have said, "'Plato is a waste of time.'"[23]

Yet, as commentators insist, Diogenes is a *parhesiast,* that is, one committed to speaking the truth.[24] According to ancient sources, he regards money as the source of evil, endures a life of poverty, commits indecent acts that can be discreetly referred to as those people do not perform in public, goes barefoot and sleeps in tubs, a style that has been described as a return to nature. He is reputed to have ordered Alexander the Great not to stand between him and the sun thereby displaying a quality of soul that Alexander admits to having envied.[25] Contemptuous of laws and lawgivers, Diogenes polemicizes against rulers and even in Hades continues to make a pest of himself

---

21. Gilles Deleuze, *What is Philosophy?* (New York: Columbia University Press, 1994), 64–65.

22. Luis E. Navia, *Classical Cynicism: A Critical Study* (Westport, Conn.: Greenwood Press, 1996), 94.

23. Ibid., 111.

24. Ibid., 103.

25. Ibid., 97.

by mocking dead kings. When asked where he was from, he is reputed to have replied: "I am a citizen of the world," a cosmopolitan, thus envisioning a single social space.[26]

According to contemporary German culture critic Peter Sloterdijk, author of *The Critique of Cynical Reason*,[27] Diogenes was the Ur-hippie and proto-Bohemian of the ancient world. When Diogenes is portrayed in ancient sources as one who is virtuous and rational, what is meant is that he illuminates the sham of law and custom,[28] a description that gives rise to the famous image of his holding a lamp and searching for an honest man. Still another tale reports his capture by pirates in the Aegean Sea who sell him as a slave, a status he promptly reverses by becoming the tutor of his master's sons, training them in endurance. His life may be summed up by the epitaph carved on the pillar that, along with a statue of a dog in Parian marble, stands over his grave:

> Tell me, Oh Dog! Who is the man whose monument thou art guarding? He is no one but the Dog himself? Diogenes indeed! . . . He was a man from Sinope. He who used to live in a tub? Yes, indeed, he himself! But now in his death, he lives among the stars![29]

For Nietzsche, the life of Diogenes is exemplary, in that the lives of cynics "recognize the animal, the commonplace, the rule in themselves . . . that itch which makes them talk of themselves and their like before witnesses,—[so that] sometimes they even wallow in books as in their own dung."[30] Because cynicism replicates the behavior of ordinary

---

26. Ibid., 100.

27. Vol. 40 of *Theory and History of Literature* (trans. Michael Eldred; Minneapolis: University of Minnesota Press, 1987).

28. Heinrich Niehues-Probsting, "The Modern Reception of Cynicism: Diogenes in the Enlightenment," in Branham and Goulet-Caze, *The Cynics*, 361.

29. Louis Navia, *Classical Cynicism*, 81.

30. Friedrich Nietzsche, *Beyond Good and Evil* (trans. Walter Kaufmann; New York: Vintage Books, 1966), 26, 38.

folk whom he often belittles, Diogenes goes on to say that "cynicism is the only form in which base souls approach honesty and the higher man must listen closely then to every coarse or subtle cynicism."[31]

The image of Diogenes may figure in Nietzsche's famed depiction of the madman who lights a lantern in the bright morning hours, crying out in the marketplace, "Where is God?" and who answers his own question with the claim, "God is dead." This image was first placed in a theological perspective by Tertullian, who valorized the metaphor of light and praised Diogenes' search with a lamp in broad daylight in contrast to the heretic Marcion, who lost the light of faith. For Nietzsche the lantern uncovers what he sees as the pointlessness of the quest for transcendence.[32] The anecdote can be read as a cynical parody of a parody, the madman displacing Diogenes of Sinope who, in turn, referred to himself as Socrates gone mad.[33]

May we not ask whether Nietzsche's cynicism undoes itself to become a new swooning, a cynicism that protests rationality in the name of a new ecstasy? In his postmodern work inspired by Nietzsche, Peter Sloterdijk argues that the present age is characterized by a diffuse but pervasive suspicion of social and political institutions. The distrustfulness of today's cynic does not express itself in the visibly eccentric but morally purposive gestures of Diogenes, whom Sloterdijk admires. Instead, he argues, the contemporary cynic is simply attuned to society's mores: "Cynicism is the universally widespread way in which enlightened people see to it that they are not taken for suckers." Thus, the enlightened or wised-up cynic understands the emptiness of his position but sees himself as merely complying with circumstances so that for him, "cynicism is enlightened false consciousness."[34] Contemporary cynicism succeeds in outfoxing moral ideologies as well as the critique of such ideologies because it is aware of its falsity. The cynicism of the present merely reappropriates the rationality of the Enlightenment that Sloterdijk sees as doomed. "To

---

31. Ibid.
32. Branham and Goulet-Caze, *The Cynics,* 361.
33. Ibid., 362.
34. Ibid., 5.

continue enlightenment means to be prepared for the fact that everything that in consciousness is mere morality will lose out against the
unavoidable amoralism of the real."[35] For Sloterdijk, the joylessness
of this false cynicism must be replaced by the higher kynicism of the
ancients, by the world-affirming cynicism of Nietzsche, by the swoon
of ecstasy.[36] His stance can be interpreted as the affirming of a negation, the negation of contemporary cynicism by way of another cynicism, one whose strategy is that of disruption. It is this notion of
cynicism that enters into postmodern artworks as commentary and
critique, thus as a kind of disfiguring of what the artwork represents.
The swooning of the Romantic is broken by a cynical consciousness
now built into the artwork itself. Must all of this, one might ask, lead
to philosophical nihilism and psychological despair?

SWOONING CYNICS AND THE WORK OF ART

Can the gasp of the swooner before the beauty of the artwork be
recovered in an age of suspicion? Or does the challenge of the cynic
call the swooner's vision of art to order by recalling the world "outside," the iniquities and atrocities of the present age? But if art is to
be schooled by moral concerns, can art avoid falling into the contemporary didacticism of Socialist Realism or into the pseudo-heroics of
Fascist kitsch? Can the beauty of the artwork be brought into question by a good that transcends it, incorporate that good, perhaps
even that which is ugly, without ceasing to be a work of art?

Consider first that the artwork is a presentation of images and that
images are a substitute for the being of a thing. As such, the image is a
doubling of reality. In ordinary recollection, I am aware of an object in
its absence but, in art, I am confronted with a substitute, a tableau,
even when the artwork is abstract and does not purport to represent
the real directly. Both artist and viewer under the sway of the image

---

35.   Ibid., 82.

36.   Throughout his work Sloterdijk changes the spelling from cynicism
to kynicism when speaking positively of the ancient version of cynicism.

are inundated by pure sensation that promotes a forgetting of the world itself. Does the "Ah" of the swooner then require the prose of criticism, the language of the cynic, to call attention to the world? Consider French culture critic Jean Baudrillard's caustic analysis of the historico-cultural nexus from which the artwork emerges, a world he perceives as the flotsam and jetsam of the past. History, he protests, refuses to come to an end but resurfaces as a waste product. Baudrillard writes:

> We have to come to terms with the idea that everything that was not biodegradable or exterminable is today recyclable. . . . We shall not be spared the worst—that is History will not come to an end—since the leftovers . . . communism, ethnic groups, conflicts, ideologies are indefinitely recyclable. What is stupendous is that nothing has really disappeared.[37]

Can there be artworks that do not require an accompanying cynical explanation such as that of Baudrillard, works that are self-explanatory, cynical in the manner of Diogenes? Can the artist as cynic not create assemblages of found objects, of the detritus of the past as exemplified in the art of Robert Rauschenberg, or culture-collages, as it were, that unsay one another as depicted in the works of Anselm Kiefer? Or consider artist C. F. G. Boggs's replicas of British and American paper money that he claimed to find beautiful. Like Diogenes who defaced the currency of Sinope, Boggs was accused of counterfeiting while the counterfeit notes, Boggs's bills, soared in value in the art market.[38] Such art requires no cynical prose supplement for the discursive elaboration of the tension between protest and artistic expression.

---

37. Jean Baudrillard, *The Illusion of the End* (trans. Chris Turner; Stanford: Stanford University Press, 1992), 27.

38. I am indebted for the account of Boggs and the role of money as artwork to Mark C. Taylor, *Disfiguring: Art, Architecture, Religion* (Chicago: University of Chicago Press, 1992), 158–63.

It can be argued further that the creation of innumerable copies of a work constitutes a cynical gesture. Philosopher Walter Benjamin, in an essay written in 1936 (thus antedating the advent of computer-generated images), maintained that in the age of mechanical reproduction copies of artworks jeopardized the authority of the original. The passing of time between its creation and the present that determines whether an artwork is original, what Benjamin called its aura, cannot be transmitted by the copy. Although reproduction had long been possible through other techniques such as engraving or wood-cutting, new technologies allow for the production of unprecedented quantities.[39] But the fact of reproduction itself in the culture of the replica can be integrated into the artwork as a critique of reproduction by introducing multiple identical images for which there is no original into the work's visual surface. Consider Andy Warhol's copies of familiar objects from soup cans to likenesses of the Mona Lisa that remind the viewer of the role of the replica in the commodification of the world. The cloned objects of the world enter the artwork as an outside that is inside and an inside that extends outward in a stream of objects. While remanding critique to the artwork itself, the viewer is still drawn into an overwhelming field of color and shape.

THEOLOGIES OF RAPTURE, THEOLOGIES OF PROTEST

Can theological thinking overwrite or reinscribe in its own language(s) the conversation between Diogenes the cynic and the Romantic artist? Recall that the visual artwork consists of images and images may be obliterated, but that an image may be dislodged without being destroyed by a process of erasure through which it remains as an absent presence in the work. Such an artwork is not simply a palimpsest, in which a new work is physically painted over an older one, rendering previous images invisible, but rather one in which

---

39. Walter Benjamin, "The Work of Art in the Age of Mechnical Reproduction," in *Illuminations* (trans. Harry Zohn; New York: Schocken Books, 1969), 217–52.

images are overlaid in another way. To understand how erasure works it must be seen in the context of the trace, a concept that has been explicated in what is by now a tradition from Heidegger to Derrida. Traces are not signs; signs are transparent in that they reveal their objects, whereas traces cannot be integrated into the order of the world. Instead, traces are not visible as such but mark a transcendence that is present in absence. The effort to coerce an absent image into appearing assures its loss; it can only be glimpsed in and through the images that are present. The images that are there may not dislodge the absent or hidden images but rather help to continue their influence.

To see this, consider again Caspar David Friedrich's painting of the man poised on the cliff, with his back toward the viewer, gazing at the infinite expanse of sea "formless, exhibiting no purpose," that we may interpret as an attempt to represent what cannot be represented, the sublime in Kant's sense. Were an artist of today to paint in the manner of Friedrich, we would be likely to dismiss such work as sentimental. However, a 1961 painting by Michaelangelo Pistoletto, *Man Seen from the Back: The Present.*[40] seems to imprint a postmodern mark upon Friedrich's painting. Pistoletto's figure, his back to the viewer, is dressed in a business suit, hands in his trouser pockets. In place of storm and sea, the man stares into a dark void. Shadowy figures, ghost-like white and red patches of light, emerge from this black background that functions like the tain of a mirror, its dark unreflective surface making its reflecting surface possible. Pistoletto writes: "Man has always attempted to double himself as a means of attempting to know himself. And part of man's mind has always remained attached to the reproduction of himself."[41] Yet the spots of light are not pictorial replicas of the man but vague incandescent shapes.

Suspended between representation and abstraction, the painting oscillates between the concrete and the conceptual. Pistoletto writes: "These two presences of myself were the two lives that were at one

---

40. See Taylor, *Disfiguring,* Plate 28.
41. Ibid., 281.

and the same time tearing me in two and calling me to the task of their unification."[42] Have we then, with Pistoletto's man seen from the back, returned to Romantic inwardization, to a pristine immersion in feeling? Does Pistoletto's statement not reinscribe a form of Romanticism criticized by Nietzsche when he says: "A romantic is an artist whose great dissatisfaction with himself makes him creative—who looks away, looks back from himself and from his world"?[43] Or does the art of Pistoletto both express and transcend this dissatisfaction? Is not "every critique [a] pioneering work on the pain of the times (*Zeitschmerz*) and a piece of exemplary healing?" as Sloterdijk asks.[44]

What has theology to gain from the depiction of an artwork as a system of traces, of images that are nested inside one another? Theologically understood, the trace is the mark of the sacred that has disrupted or passed through the beautiful. One must know how to read or rather not to read traces, how to remain attentive to them. There is in the trace the suggestion of a "more," of something uncontainable in language.

Consider once more the position of the interpreter who holds that Gen 1:31 attests the purposiveness in the order of creation and that of the interpreter who is struck by its pristine beauty. The latter might be moved to adopt Nietzsche's words: "Play, the useless—as the ideal of him who is overfull of strength, as 'childlike.' The childlikeness of God *pais paizon* (a child playing)."[45] Could such a world not be "a work of art that gives birth to itself" as Nietzsche thought? Still is there an Augustinian text, a text under erasure, nested in this excessiveness that reads: "Since then Thou fillest heaven and earth, do they contain thee? Or as they contain thee not, dost thou fill them and yet there remains something over. . . . Is it that Thou art wholly everywhere while nothing contains thee?"[46]

---

42. Ibid.

43. Nietzsche, *The Will to Power* 844, 445.

44. Sloterdijk, *Critique of Cynical Reason,* xxxvi.

45. Nietzsche, *The Will to Power* 796 and 797, 419.

46. Augustine, *Confessions,* Bk. I, chap. 3, in *Basic Writings of Saint Augustine* (ed. Whitney Oates; trans. J. G. Pilkington; New York: Random House, 1948), 4.

The beauty of the artwork solicits this excessiveness by directing attention away from itself:

> By the very beauty of his work, the artist somehow beckons the spectator, instead of fixing his eyes wholly on the beauty of the work he has made, to pass over this beauty and to look in fondness at him who made it . . . as one who hears the [words but loses] what is most important, [must pass to] the meaning of which the words are merely the signs.[47]

Yet how does one know when one has found that of which the word "gives sign?" Are the interpreters of Gen 1:31 not poised before a swirl of traces: Nietzsche in Augustine, Augustine in Nietzsche, cynics and swooners in endless conversation?

---

47. Augustine, *On Free Choice of the Will*, XVI, 168 (trans. Anna S. Benjamin and L. H. Hackstaff; Indianapolis: Library of Liberal Arts, 1964), 74.

Index

Abgar, 37–39, 44, 46–47, 50, 52, 54–57, 59

Abu Qurrah, Theodore. *See* Theodore Abu Qurrah

Adam, 60

Aegean Sea, 78

aesthetics, 40, 41n, 58, 60, 66–67, 74
   Christian, 36, 38, 62–63
   origin of, 2
   psycho-philosophical, 40
   religious, 62
   of sensation, 4
   theological, 40, 47, 61–62

Alexander the Great, 77

Ananias, 50

Andrew of Crisi, 60

anthropology, 39
   theological, 41

aporia, 5, 23, 25

appetition, 19

Aquinas. *See* Thomas Aquinas

Aristotle, 10–26, 28, 34, 49, 68–69
   De Anima, 10, 19, 20, 22, 28, 29

art, 2, 51n, 61, 63, 67, 70, 72
   as experienced, 1, 4
   and nature, 66
   process of, 46, 50
   work of, 27, 40, 61, 72, 80–82, 84
   See also aesthetics

the artist, 37–39, 42, 45–46, 50, 53, 57, 59–60, 64, 80–81, 83–85
   definition of, 73, 75
   role of, 47, 72

Augustine, 14, 19, 31, 40, 51n, 56, 84–85
   Confessions, 39

Balthasar, 6, 52, 62

Barlam, 51n

Barth, Karl, 41n

Basil, 50, 51n

Baudrillard, Jean, 81

the beautiful, 2, 6, 36, 39, 40, 43n, 45, 51n, 58–62, 67, 70
   as experienced, 1
   in Kant, 5, 74

Bede, 31

Being, 11, 30, 49

Benjamin, Walter, 81

body, 9–13, 18, 20–21, 29, 34, 43, 55–56, 58, 60, 70; *see also* flesh

Boggs, C. F. G., 81

Boileau, Nicolas, 4

Brentano, Franz, 14, 29

Burke, Edmund, 4

Cappadocian fathers, 59

Carneades, 75

Cassian, John, 56

chiasmus, 33, 41n

Christ Jesus, 8, 17, 32, 38, 41, 41n, 46–49, 53–55, 59, 64–65
   beauty of, 43, 43n, 52, 55
   crucifixion of, 41n
   dual nature of, 56
   first icon of, 36–38, 43, 45
   image of, 39, 40, 42, 50, 57, 62, 65
   as pantocrator, 46, 52
   perfection in, 58

Christianity, 34, 36, 40, 70, 73

Christology, Chalcedon, 48

Chrysostom, John, 64

cognition, 66; *see also* re-cognition